RABBIT FOOD

103 PLANT BASED RECIPES
BY GIANNA CIARAMELLO

My only focus each day is to be myself, live my true passions, inspire greater health and wear my soul shamelessly with strength and grace.

KRISTINA CARRILLO BUCARAM

RABBIT FOOD

RABBIT FOOD

Just a hungry bunny with a love for plant based foods who wants to share her recipes with each & every one of you.

Gianna Ciaramello
Author of Rabbit Food

Design & Layout by Gianna Ciaramello

All Photographs by Gianna Ciaramello

Thank you, Clara Pignatello, my Nana. Although you may not understand what a plant based lifestyle is, you are the main reason I am invested in food.

Thank you to my mother, Cora Ciaramello, who encouraged me in the kitchen mixing & cleaning green beans at two years old.

This journey began with my Nana, mom & me, three generations of women. We lived together, we cooked together, & we grew together.

Our daily rituals have flourished & enabled me to help myself so that I can help others. Such has welcomed beautiful friendships, unconditional love & lots of laughs.

I hope this book makes you smile.

FEATURED FOODIES

Donna Sammak *(Pgs 200-201)*

A loving mother & adventurous soul with a huge heart. I wish I could have known you & could have experienced your creations. Although you are not here to see this I am honored to share a piece of you in this book. Thank you for all you have done & for creating memories around your dishes.

Michaela *(Pgs 52,53 & 96,97)*

Michaela is a food stylist, recipe creator, photographer & writer for her blog ElaVegan. She has one of the biggest hearts & has rescued numerous animals. Michaela is from Germany but resides in the Dominican Republic & enjoys being creative in the kitchen & eating healthy vegan food. This girl is amazing & I am so proud to have her in this book, she really means a lot to me.

elavegan.com

@elavegan

Natasha Najjar *(Pgs 144-145)*

Natasha is a genuine & special person that I am so thankful to know. She is crazy talented & puts so much heart & soul into her dishes. She hopes to evolve her blogging into a business as well as develop a youtube channel & other upcoming projects!

@countcolorsnotcalories

Michelle Gerrard-Marriott *(Pgs 168-175)*

My dear friend, fellow foodie, beautiful soul. I am inspired by you, in awe of your creations & honored to know you. It means so much to me to be able to feature you in my first plant based cookbook. Michelle is the owner of The Vibrant Kitchen & Home.

the-vibrant-kitchen.com
@thevibrantkitchen

Carley McConkey CNP *(Pgs 44 & 91-93)*

Carley McConkey is a Toronto-based holistic nutritionist that focuses on women's health. She has a passion for healthy cooking using plant-based, whole-food and seasonal recipes using as many organic, local produce as possible. She believes in the healing power of food and that each individual is unique in their journey to optimal health.

@truenorth.wellness

CONTENTS

making bread | My Nana, my brother Angelo & me

Me preparing green beans at 2 years old

My mom & me frosting a cake

My brother & me mixing

INTRODUCTION

RABBIT FOOD is a plant based cook book filled with plant based recipes & raw foods.

WHAT DOES IT MEAN TO BE PLANT BASED?

Plant based food is derived strictly from plants, with no animal products present. The foundation of this lifestyle & diet contains the essentials for healthy eating, fruits, vegetables, whole grains, & legumes.

Health played a huge role in my life & I always wanted what was best for my body. It was only a matter of time until I discovered a plant based diet.

HOW DID IT START?

When I was just two years old my mom used to pull a chair up to the counter & put me in charge of preparing string beans. I would stand on the chair & snap the ends off for her with the biggest smile on my face. It was a simple task, but the beginning of something much bigger.

I have loved food with all of my heart since I was a little girl & cooking has been part of me since a very young age. Some of my most cherished memories stem from the times I have spent in the kitchen with Nana & my mom.

Throughout my adolescence I had a hormonal imbalance. Embarrassing abnormal hair growth, elevated testosterone levels & a general hormonal imbalance left me feeling moody, bloated & suffering from eczema & other various allergies. Adolescence is hard enough & I was a mess. I cured myself with a plant based diet & lifestyle & today my blood work is normal.

I WAS ALWAYS A HUNGRY BUNNY

I grew up in the kitchen. My after school activities consisted of making fresh pasta & baking bread. Quality of ingredients was everything & owning my first apron was a rite of passage. Despite my gluten free attempts it made no difference what type of pasta or bread I ate & this was a relief to my Nana. She may not be able to understand what it means to be plant based, however so long as I could eat pasta all was right in the world. In her eyes the Mediterranean diet is certainly more superior to American cuisine.

Kristina Carrillo-Bucaram | fullyraw.com   *Dr. Thomas Lodi | drthomaslodi.com*

As time went on I became more curious about food & health. I craved creativity in the kitchen & I was ready to help others with similar things that I had resolved with a plant based diet & lifestyle.

I did more research & I began to gravitate towards health food advocate Kristina Carrillo-Bucaram & Integrative Oncologist Dr. Thomas Lodi.

Dr. Thomas Lodi & Kristina Carrillo-Bucaram are both fully raw vegans, meaning their diets consist strictly of raw plant based foods. This concept of not ingesting cooked food was intriguing to me & immediately I needed to know more.

Connecting with these people has been a major pivot point in my journey, I instantly found myself drawn to their philosophies & methods of healing. Kristina & Dr. Lodi spend their lives working to make an impact in the health community by educating people about making healthier decisions.

With wellness centers in Thailand & Arizona, Dr. Thomas Lodi specializes in metabolic medicine, philosophy, integrative oncology & is a certified nutrition specialist. While Kristina is the leading visionary in the raw movement & pioneer in the local, organic food co-operative movement of Houston, Texas. Rawfully Organic is her co-op where you can stock up on local & organic fruits & vegetables.

Upon the discovery of these influencer's my interest in mecicine, anatomy & wellness eventually came full circle. I connected, on a more personal level, to Dr. Thomas Lodi & began to understand more about healing & the realities of how your lifestyle directly affects your overall health.

WHAT IS MY GOAL?

My passion for helping others soon evolved into finding a way to spread health & positivity in the least intimidating way. Through helping myself I gained the ability to help others. I've been an empathetic person for as long as I can remember & that was amplified when I changed my lifestyle & started taking care of myself.

I have become more aware of how my decisions directly affect the world & others around me. I've always given more of myself then I should but I have found a new way to harness that into something positive & that is why I began this journey. I thrive on the world around me & making people happy & that's all I need. From the experience gained participating in the health food community I have noticed that terms like "plant based" & "vegan" have become controversial & emotionally charged topics for many people. My goal is to neutralize these stigmas & have plant based become synonymous with simply living a healthy life.

The kitchen is my safe place where I feel I can really express myself without judgment. Growing up in the kitchen with my Nana & my mom has developed with me over my lifetime & I would love to some day implement a similar tradition into my home. Three generations preparing quality food together, coming together & working together.

I've learned that coming together & expressing ourselves with food & loved ones is the most neutral way to incorporate more healthy habits into our every day lives & that is what this book is meant for.

Spill on the pages, wrinkle them, take notes, add ingredients but most of all bring these recipes into the heart of your homes & make your own memories throughout the process of creating every single recipe.

HAZELNUT MILK & MEAL

INGREDIENTS

2 C Hazelnuts

2 Dates

1 ½ -2 C Water

INSTRUCTIONS

1. Soak the nuts & Dates overnight in enough water to cover them completely. In the morning strain the liquid & add fresh water along with the nuts & dates to your Vitamix, blend on high until the nuts are completely crushed.

2. Grab a piece of cheesecloth & a fine strainer & begin straining out the liquid. I begin by pressing the mixture through a fine strainer, then once I get enough liquid from that process I switch to the cheesecloth.

3. Slowly, begin to squeeze out liquid until you have extracted as much as you can.

4. This recipe yields 2 C of Hazelnut Milk & ½ C of Hazelnut Meal.

HOMEMADE OAT FLOUR

INGREDIENTS

2 C of Oats

INSTRUCTIONS

1. Add the Oats to your blender &
blend on high speed until a flour forms.

THOUSAND ISLAND DRESSING

INGREDIENTS

2-4 Tbs Pickle Juice

1 Dill Pickle

½ C Hampton Creek Mayo

3-6 Tbs Organic Ketchup

½-1 Tbs Horseradish (optional)

½-1 Tbs Spicy Brown Mustard (optional)

INSTRUCTIONS

1. Add all of your ingredients to a bowl.

2. Whisk until smooth & creamy.

3. Store in the fridge & enjoy within
4 days.

DILL PICKLE RANCH DRESSING

INGREDIENTS

½ C Cashews

¼ C Sunflower Seeds

½ Fresh Cucumber

¼ C Olive Oil

2 tsp Apple Cider Vinegar

5 Sprigs of fresh Dill

2 Sprigs of fresh Basil

2-3 Tbs Pickle Juice or sub water

1 Fresh Pickle Spear

1 Garlic Clove

INSTRUCTIONS

1. Add all of your ingredients to your Vitamix blender.

2. Blend on high until smooth & creamy

3. Store in the fridge & enjoy with salads, sandwiches, or as a dip with fresh veggies. This dressing lasts 3-4 days.

*Side Note : Apple Cider Vinegar can be purchased at any major super market chain as well as health food stores.

CREAMY ASIAN DRESSING

INGREDIENTS

1 C Sunflower Seeds

⅓-¼ tsp Salt

2 Tbs Nutritional Yeast

1 Clove of Garlic

2 Tbs Hemp Seeds

2 Tbs Matt's Kimchi Liquid

2 Tbs Liquid Aminos

INSTRUCTIONS

1. Add all of your ingredients to your Vitamix blender.

2. Blend on high until smooth & creamy

3. Store in the fridge & enjoy with salads, sandwiches, or as a dip with fresh veggies. This dressing lasts 3-4 days.

*Side Note : Nutritional Yeast can be purchased at any major super market chain as well as health food stores. Any Kimchi liquid will suffice if you cannot get your hands on this specific brand.

COCONUT BACON

INGREDIENTS

2-3 C of Shaved Coconut

1-2 Tbs Coconut Aminos

1-2 Tbs Maple Syrup

Parchment Paper

INSTRUCTIONS

1. Preheat your oven to 350° & apply your parchment paper to your baking pan.

2. Toss around all of the ingredients & then lay the coconut on parchment paper.

3. Allow the coconut to toast for 10-15 minutes carefully tossing it around so it doesn't burn.

*Side Note : Coconut Aminos can be purchased at health food stores. An alternative for this would be soy sauce.

RAW MAYO

INGREDIENTS

¼ C Water

¼ C Olive Oil

1 C Cashews

3 Tbs Lemon Juice

1 ¼ tsp Mustard Powder

1 tsp Apple Cider Vinegar

¼ tsp Salt

⅓ C Sunflower Seeds

INSTRUCTIONS

1. Add all of your ingredients to your Vitamix blender.

2. Blend on high until everything is smooth. If you need to add more liquid to the mixture then go ahead & add some while the mixture is blending.

*Side Note : Apple Cider Vinegar can be purchased at any major super market chain as well as health food stores.

COCONUT WHIPPED CREAM

INGREDIENTS

1 Can of Coconut Cream

3-4 Tbs Maple Syrup

INSTRUCTIONS

1. Open the can of coconut cream & remove the cream. You will not be using the liquid for this recipe so you may reserve that for something else.

2. Add the maple syrup to the coconut cream & whip with an electric mixer on high until fluffy.

3. Serve with desserts or on cakes.

CHIPOTLE MAYO

INGREDIENTS

½ C Vegan Mayo

2-3 Tbs Chipotle in Adobo Sauce

Salt & Pepper to taste

Lime Juice Optional

INSTRUCTIONS

1. Add all of your ingredients to a mixing bowl. Take the liquid from the chipotle in adobo sauce & add it in.

2. If you are sensitive to spice then taste as you add the chipotle sauce, you want to be sure to not make this sauce too spicy.

3. Whisk until incorporated, serve with burgers, sandwiches & as a sauce.

TAHINI DRESSING

INGREDIENTS

2-3 Tbs Tahini

2 Tbs Coconut Aminos

1 Tbs Liquid Smoke

2 Tbs Lemon Juice

1/3 C Hot Water

INSTRUCTIONS

1. In a small bowl add tahini, coconut aminos, liquid smoke, & lemon juice.

2. Begin to slowly whisk in your hot water, this helps thin out the mixture.

3. Serve with a nice salad. This recipe was inspired by Kate Flowers.

*Side Note . Coconut Aminos can be purchased at health food stores. An alternative for this would be soy sauce.

OVEN ROASTED RADISHES

INGREDIENTS

Radishes

Rosemary

Olive oil

Salt & Pepper

INSTRUCTIONS

1. Preheat your oven to 350°

2. Add on some of your radishes & drizzle them with olive oil, fresh rosemary & salt & pepper.

3. Roast for 30-45 minutes.

TURMERIC ROASTED POTATOES

INGREDIENTS

1 Yellow Onion, chopped

1 Tbs Garlic Powder

½-1 Tbs Oregano

½-1 Tbs Dried Parsley

5 cups Organic Potatoes (I used Yukon Gold)

½ Tbs Turmeric Powder

3-4 Tbs olive oil

Black Pepper to Taste

INSTRUCTIONS

1. Preheat oven to 350-375°, depending on your oven. Line a baking sheet with parchment paper, this ensures an easier cleanup.

2. In a gallon Zip-lock bag combine all of the ingredients & shake the bag to combine everything until all of the potatoes are well-coated.

3. Pour potatoes onto the baking sheet & bake for 35-40 minutes, tossing occasionally.

ROASTED TOMATOES

INGREDIENTS

2 C of Fresh Vine Ripe Cherry tomatoes
(feel free to use any type of tomato)

Olive Oil

Pink Himalayan Salt

Parchment Paper

INSTRUCTIONS

1. Begin by preheating your oven to 400°, apply parchment paper to a sheet pan & set aside.

2. Start by slicing your tomatoes & place cut side up onto the parchment paper. Drizzle with olive oil & add Salt to taste.

3. Bake for 20 minutes, your kitchen will smell divine.

FAST RIPE BANANAS

INGREDIENTS

Bananas that are not ripe yet

INSTRUCTIONS

1. Preheat your oven to 300°

2. Lay out your bananas on a lined baking sheet, you want to be sure to put parchment paper down because they will leak!

3. Place them in the oven for about 40 minutes. The skin will turn black which will indicate that they are done.

4. Remove & allow them to cool before using them. This is great for if you want to make banana bread but do not have any ripe bananas!

OVEN ROASTED CARROTS

INGREDIENTS

Carrots

Rosemary

Olive oil

Salt & Pepper

INSTRUCTIONS

1. Preheat your oven to 350°

2. Add on some of your carrots & drizzle them with olive oil, fresh rosemary & salt & pepper.

3. Roast for 30-45 minutes.

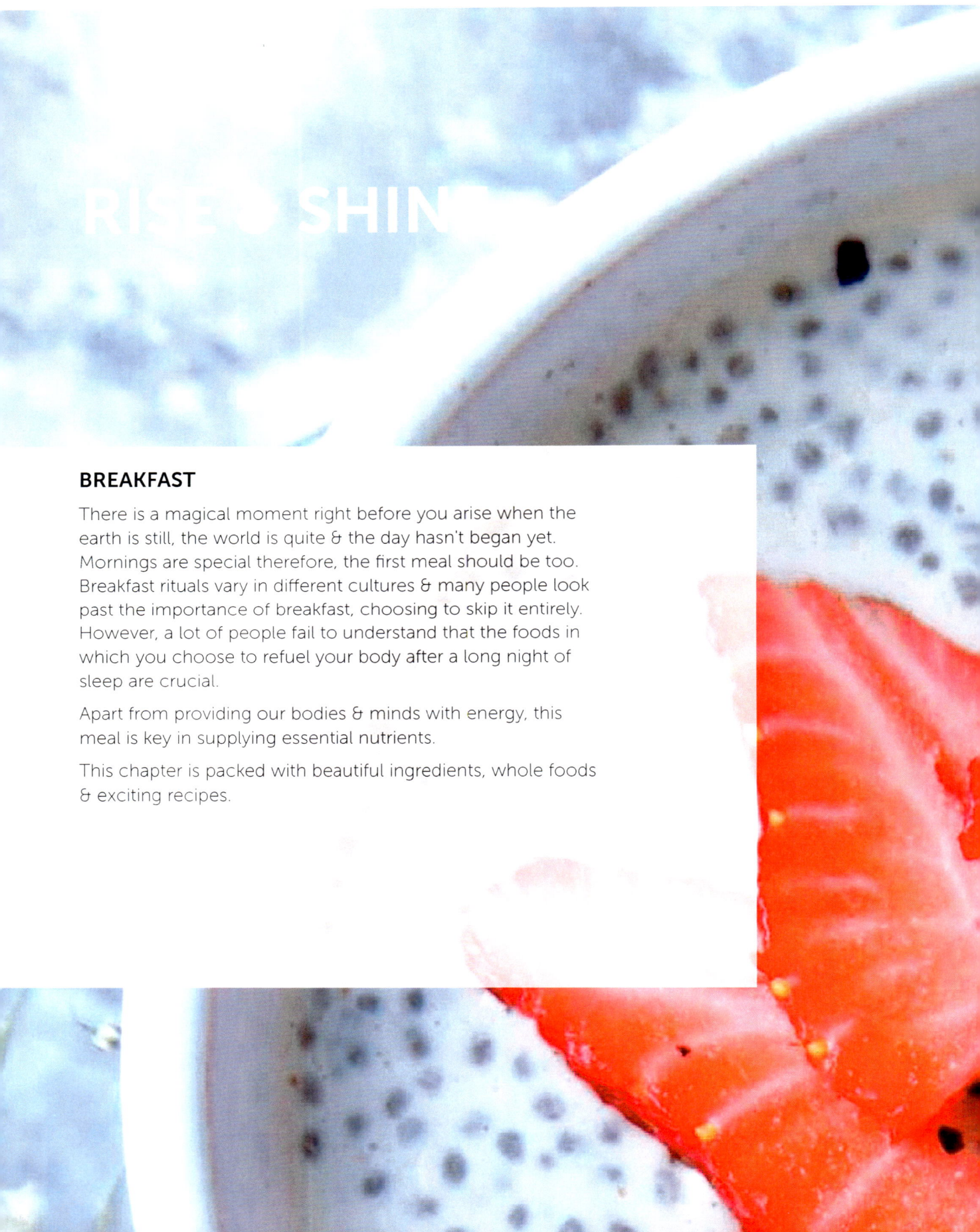

BREAKFAST

There is a magical moment right before you arise when the earth is still, the world is quite & the day hasn't began yet. Mornings are special therefore, the first meal should be too. Breakfast rituals vary in different cultures & many people look past the importance of breakfast, choosing to skip it entirely. However, a lot of people fail to understand that the foods in which you choose to refuel your body after a long night of sleep are crucial.

Apart from providing our bodies & minds with energy, this meal is key in supplying essential nutrients.

This chapter is packed with beautiful ingredients, whole foods & exciting recipes.

APPLE CINNAMON OATMEAL

Prep Time: 5 min | Total Time: 15 min | Serves: 1 Hungry Bunny

No one can underestimate the smell of an apple pie. Smell is such an irreplaceable sense that can truly transport you in time & our olfactory system holds some of the deepest emotional triggers. But we can't have pie for breakfast which is why I have created this Apple Cinnamon Oatmeal. The apples add such a rich sweetness to the oats & the cinnamon warms everything up leaving you feeling like you are slicing into a fresh piece of pie with each & every scoop.

INGREDIENTS

1 Fuji Apple

½ -1 C of Oats

Cinnamon to taste

Nut Milk of choice

1 Tbs Maple Syrup

1 Tbs Coconut Sugar

Pinch of Pink Himalayan salt

INSTRUCTIONS

1. In a small pot bring 1 C of water or nut milk & a pinch of pink Himalayan salt to a boil.

2. Stir in ½ - 1C of Oats & reduce the heat, add in ½ of the apples sliced into small pieces & allow this to cook for approximately a minute.

3. Remove from the heat & stir in the cinnamon, to taste, along with the coconut sugar.

4. Serve hot with a splash of nut milk, the rest of the apple & maple syrup.

GOLDEN MILK

Prep Time: 20 min | Total Time: 20 min | Serves: 2-3 Hungry Bunny

The first time I heard of this drink I did not imagine it being very good. I was skeptical & I imagined it tasting very bitter, medicinal & bold. This Golden Milk really surprised me, especially by making it more on the sweeter side, & I was so excited to share it!

The coconut milk used in this recipe is homemade, if you already have some then you may sub out the first 5 ingredients. If you decide to do this then I recommend adding some medjool dates separately to ensure that the milk has a sweetness to it!

INGREDIENTS

3-4 Young Thai Coconuts (Meat & Water)

2 Tbs Coconut Oil

4-8 Medjool Dates

1 tsp Vanilla + ⅛ tsp

⅛ tsp Pink Himalayan Salt

⅛ tsp Black Pepper (optional)

⅛-¼ tsp Ginger

¼ tsp Cinnamon

¼-½ tsp Turmeric (depending on how strong you want this to be)

INSTRUCTIONS

1. Carefully crack open your coconuts with either a butcher knife or a coco jack.

2. Strain out the liquid to ensure you do not get any hard pieces into the drink.

3. Scrape out all of the coconut meat this should be about 1-1 ½ C worth.

4. Add all of your other ingredients & blend on high in your Vitamix blender.

5. Taste & adjust to taste if you need to.

*Side Note: The Black Pepper is optional but contains anti inflammatory properties & is helpful in digesting the turmeric.

BEETROOT PANCAKES

Prep Time: 5 min | Total Time: 20 min | Serves: 2-3 Hungry Bunnies

Pink pancakes can make anyone smile! I would imagine myself eating these as a little girl, having tea with all of my stuffed animals & laughing like nothing else in the world mattered.

They are super light, & this recipe makes lots of little silver dollar pancakes. My personal favorite thing is the fact that the color comes from beets, & before all my beet haters judge these guys I would like to say that you co not taste the beets at all! A little goes a long way & a small wedge of beet was plenty to brighten all of these pancakes up.

INGREDIENTS

2 Ripe Bananas

1 Wedge of Beet

1 ½ C of Oats

1 Tbs Coconut Flour

Coconut Milk for blending

Vegan Dark Chocolate Chips (optional)

INSTRUCTIONS

1. Add the Oatmeal to your high speec blender or food processor. Blend until a flour forms. Add bananas, beets & liquid for blending. If the batter becomes too thin then begin mixing in coconut flour.

2. Apply coconut oil to a griddle & begin heating it up until hot.

3. Pour the batter & cook until small bubbles form & the pancake looks fairly cooked. Flip the pancakes & let them cook on alternate side.

4. Serve hot with maple syrup, agave, or molasses.

RAWNOLA BARS

I have always loved the convenience of granola bars, however they are not the most healthy snack option. Whether you are eating these as breakfast, a snack or on the go it is important to take into account the amount of sugar in them! The beauty of these granola bars is the fact that they are refined sugar free, have healthy fats, no dairy products, or processed ingredients. In fact these are totally raw!

You can customize them & adjust as you'd like, personally if I had some chocolate on hand then that would have definitely made an appearance in this recipe! These can be eaten fresh, after 2 hours of freezing or my personal favorite way after freezing them overnight. I imagine that you could also dehydrate these too & use them as a granola of some sort, no matter which way you decide they will be guaranteed to be delicious.

INGREDIENTS

1 C Hazelnut Meal (or Almond Meal)

½ C Goji Berries

½ C Pumpkin Seeds

½ C Unsweetened Shredded Coconut

½ C Buckwheat Groats

2 Tbs Black Sesame Seeds (Optional)

⅓ C GF Oats

2 Tbs Raw Honey (or sub Medjool Dates)

2 Tbs Raw Tahini

1 Tbs Vanilla (or if you are using almond meal then almond extract)

INSTRUCTIONS

1. Add all of the ingredients to your food processor.

2. Blend until well incorporated, gummy & combined.

3. Pour into a pan lined with parchment paper & place in the freezer.

4. Freeze for at least 2 hours or for optimal results overnight.

5. Slice & Enjoy!

COCONUT LIME SMOOTHIE *Carley McConkey*

INGREDIENTS

1 Frozen Banana

2 Handfuls of Spinach

¾ C cubed Pineapple (if frozen, omit ice)

1 Tbs of Hemp Hearts

Juice of 1 Lime

⅓ C of Light Coconut Milk

3 Ice Cubes & just a splash of Coconut Water.

INSTRUCTIONS

1. Add all of the ingredients to your high speed blender & blend until smooth. I garnished mine with homemade granola, hemp hearts, lime zest & coconut.

FLAX & KALE SMOOTHIE

INGREDIENTS

1 C of Kale, packed

½ C mixed frozen fruit (strawberries, banana, mango, pineapple)

1 Tbs of Flaxseed

½ Tbs Coconut Oil

Water for blending

INSTRUCTIONS

1. Add all of the ingredients to your Vitamix

2. Blend until well incorporated

Here is a great recipe for a high fat low carb green smoothie that is great for digestion. The benefits of a higher fat diet are similar to fasting. It is very important to make sure that you are getting enough healthy fats in your diet & this is a great way to start!

This smoothie is a little bit on the bitter side but it will be sure to hold you over until your next meal.

LOVE BOWL

Prep Time: 5 min | Total Time: 10 min | Serves: 1 Hungry Bunny

Sometimes we wake up & we feel like we need a little extra love & this is the perfect breakfast for that. From the dark cherries, the plump juicy figs to the little chocolate heart this Acai bowl will sweeten up your mood from the inside out!

INGREDIENTS

1 Sambazon Acai pack

1 Frozen Banana

Coconut water for blending

TOPPINGS

Golden Berries

Mulberries

Blueberries

Sunflower Seeds

Figs

Black Cherries

Strawberries

Chunky Peanut Butter

2 Chocolate Hearts

INSTRUCTIONS

1. Add the frozen banana & the Acai pack to your blender & turn it on. If you do not have a high speed blender like a Vitamix then you can begin adding coconut water so that the contents blend easier.

2. Pour into your favorite bowl & top with all of the toppings listed.

SKILLET CAKE

Prep Time: 5 min | Total Time: 20 min | Serves: 2 Hungry Bunnies

Growing up my father always made the best pancakes. Every weekend I would wake up to a familiar smell that filled the halls & made me smile This recipe was a concoction he spontaneously came up with one morning. My favorite thing about this recipe is that he made sure that it was plant based, minimal ingredients, & healthy.

INGREDIENTS

1½ C of Oatmeal

½ - 1 C Almond milk

3 Apples

1 tsp Cinnamon

1 tsp Vanilla Bean

1 Tbs Maple Syrup

INSTRUCTIONS

1. Blend the oatmeal on high until a flour forms. Add 1 apple & blend again, begin adding almond milk until batter begins to form.

2. Peel the other two apples & slice them into thin pieces.

3. Add the apples to an 8" cast iron skillet & let them caramelize & soften.

4. Once the apples soften add the maple syrup & the cinnamon.

5. The apples should begin to have a nice brown color this is when you add the batter & let it cook. This should take about 10-15 minutes.

THE WILD MERMAID

This is a mysterious cross between banana ice cream, sorbet & a smoothie. When I say the flavors are perplexing I mean they really are unpredictable. Taking your first spoon-dive you will experience minty refreshing banana ice cream, maybe a little crunch of cacao nibs. As you scoop up your next bite the familiar minty-ness may still be present, however, this time you will also have the mildly sweet dragon fruit accompanied by some chewy little devils, the golden berries

INGREDIENTS

½ Frozen Purple Dragon Fruit

Coconut Water for blending

2 Frozen Bananas

2 tsp Spirulina

Small palm full of Mint

TOPPINGS

Golden Berries

Sour Cherries

Cacao Nibs

INSTRUCTIONS

1. Begin by blending the Purple Dragon Fruit & the Coconut Water in order to create Base #1.

2. Blend Frozen Bananas, Spirulina, & Mint along with some Coconut Water to create Base #2

3. Layer the flavors in your favorite jar

4. Add the toppings & enjoy!

*Side Note: Picking mint in the rain was how I began my morning. In a small towel I gathered the little leaves soaked with drops of water & prepared them for this recipe. With all of its mystical colors & mysterious flavors I thought of nothing but mermaids.

CREPES FILLED WITH CHOCOLATE *Michaela*

Prep Time: 5 min | Total Time: 20 min | Serves: 6 Hungry Bunnies

If you crave something sweet for breakfast then make these vegan gluten free crepes next time. These also are great as an afternoon snack, Michaela loves having these as an afternoon snack because that's the time when she always crave something sweet!

INGREDIENTS

1 C Gluten Free Oat Flour

4 Tbsp Tapioca Flour/Starch

4 Tbsp Potato Starch or Corn Starch

2 Tbsp Ground Flax Seeds

1 ½ C Plant Milk (I used Coconut Milk)

1 ½ Tbsp Maple Syrup

INSTRUCTIONS

1. Process all ingredients in your food processor or just whisk them together in a bowl.

2. Heat a non-stick pan/skillet (I used a 10 inch ceramic skillet) with some oil over medium heat.

3. Pour about ¼ C of the batter into the pan, swirl the batter around to coat the pan evenly. Cook for about 2-4 minutes or until you can easily lift a side of the crepe (don't try to flip the crepe too early). After you carefully flipped the crepe, cook for a further 1-2 minutes.

4. After a while the batter will get thicker (because of the ground flax seeds), just add a little bit more plant milk.

5. Fill your crepes with a chocolate spread.

WINTER KIWI BOWL

Prep Time: 8 min | Total Time: 10 min | Serves: 1 Hungry Bunny

---

Humid & rainy summer mornings filled with lots of tea & reflection. As I sit in the sun room appreciating the moody clouds & rain pattering down I cannot help but feel a sense of gratitude for the world around me. Rain is so unappreciated, but I simply love it. I long for the days when the grumpy clouds roll in & water all of the greenery & life around me. But the most calming moment of storm is when it ends. The fresh smell of earth mixed with water, soil & air.

INGREDIENTS

1 Sambazon Acai Pack

1 Frozen Banana

½ C Frozen Strawberries

1-2 tsp Cacao Powder

1 tsp Spirulina

Nut milk for blending

TOPPINGS

Banana

Dried Mulberries

Cacao Nibs

Chia Seeds

Ground Flax Seeds

Strawberries

Spirulina

Coconut Sugar

INSTRUCTIONS

1. Blend until desired consistency is achieved.

2. Continue adding liquid based off of how the ingredients are blending.

3. Pour into your favorite bowl & add whatever toppings you'd like.

KALE BOWL

INGREDIENTS

1 Sambazon Acai Pack

1 C Frozen Strawberries

½ C Frozen Blueberries

1-2 C Chopped Kale

Coconut water for blending

TOPPINGS

Kale

Strawberries

Blueberries

Pumpkin Seeds

Ground Flax Seeds

INSTRUCTIONS

1. Blend until desired consistency is achieved.

2. If the kale is having difficulty blending then feel free to add more coconut water.

I absolutely love having greens at the start of my day & my favorite way to do it is by sneaking them into smoothies & acai bowls. Blending the greens into whatever you are eating is a great way to conceal them & get more fiber & nutrients into your diet, without having to have a salad. I love pairing greens like kale with sweeter fruits in order to hide the bitterness & create delicious options!

ALIEN WATER

This is more of an idea then a recipe. Every-time I made a juice I am guilty of quickly rinsing out the jar & calling it a day. The last time I made my Re-hydration Smoothie I was advised to fill the jar back up with water. At first I was skeptical & quite frankly nervous to have a bitter watered down "juice" but I was pleasantly surprised to have more of a flavored water that was beautiful, hydrating & vibrant.

When the we put the juice on the counter the light hit it & an alien like glow was revealed that immediately gave me the idea to name this Alien Water. So next time you finish a juice refill your jar & enjoy the remaining flavors.

A big thanks to Derek Sammak for the idea as well as the photography skills.

BLUEBERRY CHIA PORRIDGE

Prep Time: 5 min | Total Time: Overnight | Serves: 1 Hungry Bunny

I have always loved to have cream of wheat for breakfast, my mother used to make it for me on the stove & I loved everything about it. The smell, watching her stir at the stove, the texture, it truly felt like a comfort meal. If you are looking for a cozy raw breakfast option then this is perfect. This chia porridge is super creamy, rich, comforting & came highly recommended to me. I couldn't believe how much of a connection I made to this breakfast & how much it reminded me of my cream of wheat mornings with my mother.

INGREDIENTS

1-2 C Homemade Almond Milk

1 Tbs Maple Syrup

2-3 Tbs Chia seeds

Blueberries

Strawberries

¼ tsp Pink Himalayan Salt (optional)

INSTRUCTIONS

1. Pour some almond milk into a bowl

2. Add the chia seeds & whisk to incorporate.

3. At this point if you would like this to be sweet you may add the maple syrup.

4. Sprinkle in the Pink Himalayan salt & whisk again.

5. Transfer to a jar & give it another shake, place in the fridge & let it sit overnght.

6. Top with fresh fruit & enjoy.

ELA'S PANCAKES

Prep Time: 5 min | Total Time: 15 min | Serves: 2-3 Hungry Bunnies

---

Summer of 2015 I met a girl named Michaela, a recipe creator, with the biggest heart. I cannot believe where the time has gone & how much her following has grown since but one thing that has not changed is how much she inspires me. She inspires me to do as much as I can for animals while continueing to make new plant based recipes! This recipe, which I reference through out my cook book, was inspired from her & I continue to use it most times I make pancakes.

INGREDIENTS

2 Ripe Bananas

1 ½ C of Oats

1 Tbs Coconut Flour

Plant Milk of choice or Coconut Water for blending

INSTRUCTIONS

1. Add the Oatmeal to your high speed blender or food processor. Blend until a flour forms. Add bananas & liquid for blending. If the batter becomes too thin then begin mixing in coconut flour..

2. Apply coconut oil to a griddle & begin heating it up until hot.

3. Pour the batter & cook until small bubbles form & the pancake looks fairly cooked. Flip the pancakes & let them cook on alternate side.

4. Serve hot with maple syrup, agave, or molasses.

PAPAYA SORBET

INGREDIENTS

½ C of frozen Blackberries

½ of a Fresh Papaya

2-3 Tbs Lime Juice

Orange Juice or coconut water for blending

INSTRUCTIONS

1. Add all of the ingredients to your Vitamix blender.
2. Blend on high until sorbet forms
3. Pour into your favorite piece of fruit, I used the skin from my papaya.
4. Serve with whatever toppings you'd like.

Who needs a bowl when you have tropical fruit available? This is a great way to utilize all parts of the fruit while feeling like you are off on a tropical island enjoying your breakfast! There are many fruits you can use as bowls, such as coconuts & pineapples to name a few. This sorbet could also be eaten as a dessert & is a great option for a hot day.

PAPAYA SMOOTHIE BOWL

INGREDIENTS

1-2 Frozen Bananas

½ of a Papaya

½ of a Frozen Dragon Fruit

TOPPINGS

Cacao nibs

Desiccated Coconut

Raw Pumpkin Seeds

Plum

Kiwi

INSTRUCTIONS

1. Blend together the ingredients for the base

2. Top with the Cacao Nibs, Desiccated Coconut, Pumpkin Seeds, Plum & Kiwi.

I had bountiful amounts of papaya on hand & thought that I would incorporate some into my smoothie bowl. The result created a super creamy, & dreamy, sweet & floral base that really had me dying to share this recipe!

SPIRULINA BANANA ICE CREAM

This creation is everything I dreamed of. I have been so in love with the beautiful color that spirulina adds to dishes & I have been experimenting with different recipes that may benefit from spirulina. Not only is the color fun but there are so many amazing benefits to spirulina as well! Spirulina has 60% protein & is also an excellent source of vitamins A, K1, K2, B12 & iron. This super food also has 2800% more beta-carotene than carrots & 3900% more iron than spinach.

INGREDIENTS

2 Frozen Bananas

1 tsp of Spirulina

Almond Milk for blending

TOPPINGS

Golden Berries

Cacao nibs

Pumpkin Seeds

INSTRUCTIONS

1. Add the ingredients for the base to your blender & blend until smooth

2. Top with Pumpkin Seeds, Golden Berries, & Cacao Nibs.

*Side Note. For this recipe I did not use a high speed blender & I ended up adding more liquid then probably necessary. The result is much more soupy compared to if you have a Vitamix. With the Vitamix you will have the consistency of ice cream.

PEANUT BUTTER WAFFLES

Prep Time: 10 min | Total Time: 10-20 min | Serves: 2-3 Hungry Bunnies

Waffles can be quite the challenge. If the batter is not right then it burns, doesn't cook properly & just makes you mad! The waffle iron can be messy & intimidating but that doesn't mean that their not worth the work! These peanut butter waffles are sure make any peanut butter lover happy. They almost have a peanut butter & jelly type of vibe going on because of the berry sauce. I hope this is a recipe that is served hot on a beautiful weekend morning!

INGREDIENTS

½ C Rolled Oats

½ C Rice Flour

1-2 tsp Baking Powder

2 Tbs Flax seeds

2-3 Tbs Tapioca Flour

½-1 C Almond Milk

3-4 Tbs Coconut Sugar

1 bag of Frozen Mixed Berries

INSTRUCTIONS

1. Add all of these ingredients to your food processor & blend until smooth. The mixture should be creamy.

2. Heat up your waffle iron & coat liberally with coconut oil or olive oil. Slowly begin to pour in about 1/4-1/2 a cup of batter at a time.

3. Allow the waffles to cook for about 5 minutes, it may take longer depending on your waffle iron.

4. When your waffles are done spread some peanut butter in between each one.

5. Add your mixed frozen berries to a hot skillet & smash with a fork while they heat up.

6. Serve hot.

CACAO CHIA PORRIDGE

Prep Time: 5 min | Total Time: Overnight | Serves: 1 Hungry Bunny

---

If you love chocolate then this chia porridge is for you! Creamy, sweet savory, decadent & delicious, this breakfast option is sure to satisfy any sweet tooth. You are able to make this dish with almond milk however the hazelnut milk really compliments the chocolate & makes this dish taste more like a dessert then a breakfast! Think of nutella stirred into porridge, chocolate & hazelnuts are a match made in heaven! Make this for your kids, loved ones, or even on a gloomy Monday & you will be guaranteed to have the best day!

INGREDIENTS

1-2 C Homemade hazelnut milk

1 Tbs Maple Syrup

2-3 Tbs Chia seeds

1-2 Tbs Cacao Powder

Mulberries

Pumpkin Seeds

Cacao Nibs

¼ tsp Pink Himalayan Salt (optional)

INSTRUCTIONS

1. Pour some hazelnut milk into a bowl

2. Add the chia seeds & whisk together until incorporated.

3. At this point you may add the maple syrup & cacao powder, continue whisking.

4. Sprinkle in the Pink Himalayan salt & whisk again

5. Transfer to a jar & give it another shake, place in the fridge & let it sit overnight.

6. Top with pumpkin seeds, cacao nibs, mulberries & enjoy.

*Side Note: This recipe can be made with any plant milk of choice. I personally love the fusion of chocolate and hazelnut.

SUNSHINE BOWL

Prep Time: 5 min | Total Time: 10 min | Serves: 1 Hungry Bunny

---

Good Morning Sunshines, here is a great way to start off your day with a smile. I always love waking up & having breakfast with my mother. Our mornings usually consist of sitting at the counter & discussing what our days are like, then I usually make her something like this. This recipe is guaranteed to make you smile & is best if shared with someone you love!

INGREDIENTS

1 Sambazon Acai Pack

½ C Frozen Strawberries

1-2 Frozen Bananas

Almond Milk for blending

TOPPINGS

Persimmons

Pecans

Pumpkin Seeds

Ground Flax Seeds

Goji Berries

INSTRUCTIONS

1. Gather the ingredients for the base & place them in a high speed blender or food processor.

2. Blend until smooth & add the toppings.

*Side Note: If you are active & enjoy working out in the morning then this is a great pre-workout meal. Consuming fruit pre-workout is a great way to fuel & prepare your body for exercise & energize your cells.

PEACHY PEACH OATCAKES

Prep Time: 5 min | Total Time: 15 min | Serves: 2-3 Hungry Bunnies

These may look like pancakes but they are actually oatcakes. This is something new that I tried & I was super pleased with the outcome.

This recipe was inspired by taking a regular bowl of oatmeal & decided to spoon dollops of it onto a griddle. The result was thick little "cakes" that were super healthy, satisfying & unique.

INGREDIENTS

2 ripe Bananas mashed or puréed

4 Peaches mashed or puréed

1-2 C of Oat Meal + 2 Tbs

1 tsp Almond Extract

1 tsp Cinnamon

Almond Milk for blending

INSTRUCTIONS

1. Add all of your ingredients to a high speed blender & blend on high until smooth.

2. If batter is too thin, add the other 1-2 Tbs of Oat Flour.

3. Serve hot with molasses or maple syrup.

PEANUT BUTTER FREAK SHAKES

Prep Time: 5 min | Total Time: 10 min | Serves 2-3 Hungry Bunnies

Freakshakes are a monstrous fusion of smoothies & ice cream. Traditionally these shakes are packed with candies, chocolates & treats that are filled with unhealthy ingredients. The beauty of these cruelty free, banana based shakes is that they are healthy & refined sugar free. These shakes are a great breakfast & dessert option. If you are a peanut butter lover like me then these peanut butter freakshakes are guaranteed to satisfy.

INGREDIENTS

2-3 Frozen bananas

3 Tbs of PB2 Powdered Peanut Butter

Nut Milk for Blending

3-4 Tbs Raw Cocoa Powder

5 Tbs Coconut Oil that has been melted

2 Tbs Maple Syrup

OPTIONAL TOPPINGS

Brownie Bites

Jungle Peanuts

Dark Chocolate

Side Note: Don't be afraid to pile high & then top with more chocolate sauce, bits of brownie & whatever else you'd like!

INSTRUCTIONS

1. For the ice cream add all of your ingredients to your blender

2. Blend on high until thick & creamy. Then set aside & begin preparing the chocolate sauce.

3. In a food processor, blend the cocoa powder, melted coconut oil, & maple syrup until sauce begins to form.

4. Begin to layer the shakes by starting with a layer of crushed jungle peanuts, brownie bites & chocolate sauce.

5. Pour in the peanut butter & banana ice cream so the jar is filled about halfway.

6. Add more peanuts, brownie bites & chocolate sauce & then fill the rest of the jar up with the remaining ice cream.

BANANA ICE CREAM

Prep Time: 5 min | Total Time: 5 min | Serves 1-2 Hungry Bunnies

If you are able to get your hands on a Vitamix blender & you love bananas then this recipe is for you. Many people like a cold smoothie or shake & they'll add ice to their concoctions in order to chill it. You can achieve a super frosty like smoothie by freezing your bananas! Simply peel off the skin & place them into an air tight container. Freeze overnight & you are ready to go! This recipe is my personal favorite way to enjoy banana ice cream. Simple, creamy & healthy!

INGREDIENTS

4-6 Frozen Bananas

1 Passion Fruit

½ of a Vanilla Bean

Plant milk (optional)

*Side Note: You do not need to add liquid to this recipe. If you are using a Vitamix then you will absolutely be able to create an ice cream like consistency without breaking your blender or using liquid! If you do not have a Vitamix then you may shave the banana using a grater. This was a recommendation I discovered through Lina Saber.

INSTRUCTIONS

1. The night before, peel the bananas that you want to use & place them in an air tight container.

2. Place in the freezer & allow them to freeze throughout the night. This is important to ensure the bananas create the fluffy consistency you'd like.

3. In the morning grab your bananas & place them in your blender with your passion fruit & vanilla bean.

4. Blend until super fluffy & creamy.

5. Serve with more passion fruit or toppings of choice!

MAPLE PECAN FLAPJACKS

Prep Time: 8 min | Total Time: 10 -15 min | Serves:3-4 Hungry Bunnies

What a sultry looking stack of jacks! These flapjacks are so good that you w ll be eating them off of the griddle, but be careful not to burn your fingers! I highly recommend these pancakes, especially if you are feeling like you want to have a special & cozy kind of morning.

INGREDIENTS

2 C of Almond Milk

2 C of Oat Flour

¼ tsp Baking Soda

¼ tsp Baking Powder

1 Whole Banana

2 Tbs of Ground Flaxseed

2-3 Tbs of Maple Syrup or 5 Pureed Dates

Splash of Almond Extract

⅓ C Crushed Pecans (or simply only to garnish)

Generous sprinkle of Cinnamon

INSTRUCTIONS

1. Add all of the ingredients to your blender or food processor & blend until well incorporated

2. In the meantime begin to apply coconut oil to your skillet & heat it on high.

3. Once the skillet is hot reduce to low heat & spoon on your batter. Cook until the pancakes are fluffy.

4. Garnish with whatever you'd like. I used figs & some pecans.

*Side Note: If you don't have any oat flour on hand then just put oatmeal in the blender & blend until you've reached a flour consistency

SUNSHINE POPSICLES

Prep Time: 15 min | Total Time: 24 hours | Serves: 2-4 Hungry Bunnies

---

The sunsets of summer are some of the most special ones. The temperature is perfect, the lightning bugs are beginning to flutter around, everything feels right. My favor te thing growing up was running into the garage & digging through the refrigerator in search of some ice pops. They were always amazing to cool off with & I loved how icy, refreshing, & sugary they were.

These sweet, tangy pops are perfect for you & your kids to snack on during or at the end of a beautiful summer day. This is also a great way to get essential vitamins & benefits of juicing into younger tummies!

INGREDIENTS

5-6 Oranges Juiced

½ - 1 Pineapple Juiced

1 Lemon Juiced

INSTRUCTIONS

1. Juice your oranges, lemon & your pineapple.

2. If you do not want these to contain pulp you can strain the juice to remove it.

3. Pour the liquid into a Popsicle mold & place in the freezer overnight.

4. Share with your loved ones & enjoy

*Side Note: You may add chia seeds to this recipe if you are feeling more adventurous! This also will add some texture & pairs nicely with the pulp, in case you decide to leave it!

REFRESH BOWL

Prep Time: 8 min | Total Time: 10 min | Serves: 1 Hungry Bunny

---

Every day we wake up to a new day, a clean slate, a fresh start. Every day is a new adventure & another page of our stories. If you didn't like something about the you that you were yesterday, then change it.

Wake up today & be the best version of yourself that you can be. Here is a recipe for an Acai bowl that will allow you to conquer the day head on!

INGREDIENTS

1 Sambazon Acai pack

3 Apricots

1 Frozen Banana

TOPPINGS

Apricots

Strawberries

Blueberries

Figs

Dehydrated raspberries

Hemp seeds

INSTRUCTIONS

1. Blend until desired consistency is achieved

2. Top with the toppings listed, or whatever fruit you'd like & most importantly remember to smile.

MID DAY

MID DAY

There isn't always a clear line defining breakfast & lunch or late lunch & early dinner. In some cultures the meals are quite diverse & not traditionally eaten the same way as western culture. I think the best way to differentiate this meal is by thinking of it as a mid day meal, whether it consists of fruit platters, salads, sandwiches, leftovers or late breakfast.

This less formal meal can still be filled with delicious dishes & be eaten any time of day. I always enjoyed the more relaxed feel of it & I usually listen to my body. If I am still full from some fluffy pancakes I had for lunch then I opt for something lighter, & if I am ravenous then I will make myself the most delicious sandwich! But that is up to you to decide.

KALE & ROMAINE CAESAR SALAD

Prep Time: 5 min | Total Time: 5 min | Serves: 2-3 Hungry Bunny

I'll be the first one to admit that eating a salad is sometimes difficult for me. However, if it is made in a certain way then I will have no problem eating them all the time.

This is one of those salads that will get any salad lover to dig in! I love the flavor of the additional capers & they're brine, which is in the dressing. You could also use this as a dip with carrots & celery or as a spread on sandwiches & wraps.

INGREDIENTS

1 C Raw Cashews

1 tsp Mustard Powder

1 tsp White Pepper

1 Tbs Nutritional Yeast

¼ tsp Salt

½ C Capers + 2-3 Tbsp Brine

1 Lemon Juiced (2 Tbs)

3-4 Tbs Olive Oil

¼ C Sunflower Seeds (optional)

1 Tbs Hemp seeds (optional)

Capers

Tomatoes

Pumpkin Seeds

INSTRUCTIONS

1. Take your cashews, mustard powder, white pepper, nutritional yeast, salt, caper brine, lemon juice, olive oil, hemp seeds & sunflower seeds. (The hemp seeds & sunflower seeds are optional) Blend until smooth & super creamy.

2. If you'd like you can add in fresh herbs, this is optional & does change the flavors a bit.

3. Add to your greens & top with capers, tomatoes & pumpkin seeds.

RAW COLLARD WRAPS

Prep Time: 5 min | Total Time: 5 min | Serves: 1 Hungry Bunny

---

Collard wraps filled with tons of veggies, color, flavor & no meat?! I'll take 10 please! Now don't get me wrong, you guys know I love a good sandwich & I could always go for a nice wrap but these guys held up just as good & are a great healthy option!

The dates were such an out of this world addition & I think I have found a new love for my sandwich creations. It supplied an ooey gooey sweetness that complimented all of the other flavors & really mellowed out the bitterness of the veggies.

INGREDIENTS

Shredded Rainbow Carrots

Tomato

Red Onion

Strawberries

Dill

Broccoli Sprouts

Red Bell Pepper

Fresh Basil Leaves

Dates

Cashew Based Mayo

Grated Horseradish

INSTRUCTIONS

1. Get 2 massive collard leaves & remove the thick part of the stem.

2. Overlap them for extra workspace & security.

3. Spread a super generous amount of grated horseradish along the bottom, mixed with a little of a cashew based mayonnaise.

4. Add all of the veggies & carefully wrap up the collard leaf

GRILLED AVOCADO BAGEL

INGREDIENTS

Red leaf lettuce

Fresh Raw Beets

Cucumbers

Radishes

Horseradish

Dill (to taste)

2-3 Tbs Cashew Based Mayo

Fresh Pumpernickel Bagel

INSTRUCTIONS

1. Begin by toasting a fresh pumpernickel bagel

2. Spread on some of the cashew mayo & some horseradish

3. Pile high with veggies & enjoy!

*Side Note: This recipe is wonderful with cooked beets as well

Horseradish & beets are a match made in heaven, pair that with the fresh dill & cucumbers & you will have quite a lovely sandwich.

LEMON & GINGER TONIC *Carley McConkey*

INGREDIENTS

5 (2 inch) Pieces of Ginger

Juice of 2 Lemons

1 Tbs of Powdered Turmeric

A touch of Freshly Ground Pepper

¼ C of filtered water

INSTRUCTIONS

1. Blend & then strain.

2. Add 1 oz of mixture into a mug or mason jar & top with hot water. You can keep the rest of the mixture in a sealed jar in the fridge & use it over the course of 3 days. Feel free to add honey if desired.

This drink is anti-inflammatory, good for digestion, antiviral & it is sure to cure what ails ya.

COCONUT CARROT SOUP *Carley McConkey*

Prep Time: 10 min | Total Time: 15-20 min | Serves: 3-4 Hungry Bunnies

This soup is cozy, comforting, flavorful & delicious. This would be a great soup to have on a cold winter day, shared with loved ones. The creamy carrots & sweet potatoes mixed with the coconut milk make for real comfort food.

INGREDIENTS

7 Carrots Chopped

1-2 Celery Stalks

2 Tbs Coconut Oil

1 Sweet Potato

1 Onion Chopped

3 Cloves of Garlic

3 C Vegetable Stock

1 C of Water (you might want to add more)

One 15-oz can of Coconut Milk

1 ½ Tbs freshly Chopped Ginger Root

1 Tbs Curry Powder

1 Tbs of Turmeric

Salt & Pepper to taste

INSTRUCTIONS

1. Heat the coconut oil in a large pot & add onion, garlic & celery.

2. When the onions have softened, add the carrots & sweet potato & cook for another 5 minutes.

3. Pour in the stock, water, coconut milk, ginger, curry powder & turmeric.

4. Cook until the carrots & sweet potato have softened, about 10 minutes.

5. Blend & enjoy!

MEXICAN SALAD JAR

Prep Time: 15-20 min | Total Time: 30 min | Serves: 1-2 Hungry Bunnies

I needed some spice in my life today & I was craving something feisty & this "cocktail" Mexican salad absolutely hit the spot.

This is a great recipe to make for a family party or to bring to work with you. I also love using the taco meat portion of this recipe for raw burritos & raw tacos. You can even take it a step further & dehydrate it in order to give it more texture!

INGREDIENTS

1 Bell pepper

1 C of Spinach

Homemade Guacamole

Red Onion

Mushrooms

Lime

SUN DRIED TOMATO & WALNUT MEAT

½ C raw walnuts, soaked overnight

½ C Sun dried tomatoes

2 teaspoons chili powder

2 teaspoon cumin

1 clove or garlic

2 tsp chipotle powder

1 lime juiced

1 wedge of beet (optional for color)

INSTRUCTIONS

1. Blend all of the ingredients for the walnut meat until the consistency is crumbly

2. Begin to fill your jar by adding a layer of the walnut meat.

3. Pack in your favorite greens, I personally used spinach

4. Add in bell pepper, homemade guacamole, & top with mushrooms & red onion

5. Squeeze on lime juice & enjoy!

CHICKPEA CURRY *Michaela*

Prep Time: 15 min | Total Time: 25 min | Serves: 2 Hungry Bunnies

Enjoying this vegan chickpea curry made me realize how awesome comfort food is & also how much I love it. I am a huge fan of Indian food & spices. This recipe contains all my favorite ingredients, which are chickpeas, eggplant, coconut milk, rice & of course curry powder. If you combine all these ingredients you will end up with the most delicious & satisfying vegan curry as a result.

INGREDIENTS

1 15-ounce can Chickpeas, drained & rinsed

2-3 Small Eggplant or 1 big one

½ Large Onion, diced

2-3 Cloves Garlic, minced

1 C Unsweetened Coconut Milk, canned

1 Tbsp Curry Powder (you can use curry paste instead)

1 tsp Onion Powder

½ tsp Ground Cumin

¼ tsp Turmeric (optional)

¼ tsp Smoked Paprika (optional)

Salt & Pepper to taste

Cooked rice of choice

Spinach or Fresh Coriander for serving

INSTRUCTIONS

1. Chop the eggplant & onion & put them in a large pan (I use a ceramic pan & no oil) & cook on medium heat for about 5 minutes. Add the garlic & cook for a another minute.

2. Drain & rinse chickpeas & add them to the pan.

3. Add coconut milk, spices, salt & pepper to taste. Simmer for another 4 minutes.

4. Serve your curry with cooked rice of choice. Decorate with either spinach or fresh coriander. Enjoy!

GARLIC SCAPE & HERB BAGEL

Prep Time: 5 min | Total Time: 10 min | Serves: 1 Hungry Bunny

---

There is nothing like a round fluffy everything bagel. I know bagels have a bad rap but they are definitely a necessary indulgence. I love experimenting with different variations of spreads & toppings for bagels.

This combination may be my favorite one yet. Combining these ingredients & whipping them together results in an incredibly fluffy & refreshing spread.

INGREDIENTS

Everything bagel
Garlic Scapes
Fresh Dill
Fresh Picked Parsley
Kite hill Cream Cheese

INSTRUCTIONS

1. Carefully slice your everything bagel & set aside.

2. Dice up the garlic scapes, dill, & parsley.

3. Add these ingredients to a small bowl along with some Kite hill cream cheese & whip everything together with an electric mixer.

4. Spread generously on your bagel & enjoy!

*Side Note: Kite hill Cream Cheese is by far my favorite vegan cream cheese. I personally feel that unless I am making the cream cheese myself I would always prefer one that is minimally processed & full of rich flavor!

RE-HYDRATION SMOOTHIE

Prep Time: 5 min | Total Time: 5 min | Serves: 1 Hungry Bunny

---

Eating your greens is important & so is staying hydrated. Drinking a lot of water is important for skin health, hair health & overall function of the body. Being hydrated increases energy, reduces fatigue, curbs appetite, promotes weight loss, flushes out toxins, boosts your immune system, prevents cramps & sprains & improves mood overall.

I personally started increasing my water intake in order to reduce my appetite, a lot of the time when we experience feelings of hunger they are really feelings of thirst. This common mix up causes us to eat more & drink less. I love having this smoothie in the morning or mid day, it is a great way to get in your greens & to rehydrate!

INGREDIENTS

3 C Spinach

1 Whole Lemon, (rind removed)

5 Dates

1 Packed handful of Parsley

1 Cucumber

3 Celery Stalks

1 Chunk of Aloe

Water or Coconut Water

INSTRUCTIONS

1. Fill your Vitamix blender with all of your ingredients.

2. Top everything off with water or coconut water, you can fill the blender up half way or more.

3. Blend on high & serve.

KIMCHI NORI WRAP

Prep Time: 5 min | Total Time: 5 | Serves: 1 Hungry Bunny

Fermented foods were not always my thing but as time went on & my palate evolved I began to absolutely love it & crave the tanginess of it!

Kimchi can be mild to feisty, depending on the amount of kick to it. This kimchi is vegan, free of gluten, dairy, soy, fish & nut products & is made by hand by my friends Matt Volin & Fiona Lee. I was so excited to incorporate it into a dish & I thought this combination would be perfect! I love sandwiches & this is a great way to eat your favorite sandwich foods without the bread!

INGREDIENTS

Matt's Kimchi

Shredded Cucumber

Shredced Carrot

Pickled Cucumber, Daikon, Jalapeño & Ginger

Avocado

Herb Cashew Cheese spread

Purple Cabbage

INSTRUCTIONS

1. Take a sheet of NORI & lay it flat. Spread on some herb cashew cheese spread, I personally love the brand Miyoko. ̧carlic, lemon juice, flaxseed, salt, dill & blend it in a Vitamix blender.

3. Begin to pile on your purple cabbage, shredded carrots, shredded cucumber, pickled veggies, avocado & Matt's K mchi.

4. Roll up carefully & enjoy!

ASIAN SESAME ZOODLES

Prep Time: 20 min | Total Time: 30 min | Serves: 2-3 Hungry Bunnies

This is by far the easiest raw dish that I have ever made. Not only are the flavors diverse but the ingredients are minimal. Zoodles are zucchini noodles that have been created with a spiralizer, they are a great low carb replacement for pasta & add flare to a lot of raw dishes.

These noodles are light but salty & have tons of crunch. I recommend making & eating this dish in the same day to ensure the noodles do not get soggy. Photo taken by Victoria Tonno

INGREDIENTS

3 Zucchinis Spiralized

2 Carrots Spiralized (or more zucchinis)

1-2 Bell Peppers

2 Large Tomatoes

Garlic Scapes

Scallions

Raw Unhulled Sesame Seeds, I use Black sesame seeds so it looks extra fancy

1 Avocado

Braggs Liquid Aminos

INSTRUCTIONS

1. Add your spiralized veggies to a mixing bowl.

2. Toss with Braggs Liquid Aminos, to taste

3. Top with sliced tomatoes, bell peppers, garlic scapes, scallions, sesame seeds, & avocado.

*Side Note : Braggs Liquid Aminos can be purchased at any major super market chain as well as health food stores. An alternative for this would be soy sauce.

KIMCHEESE

Prep Time: 20 min | Total Time: 20 min | Serves: 1 Hungry Bunny

---

When I was growing up the grilled cheese was the king of sandwiches. I would seriously devour any amount of them that you put in front of me without batting a lash.

This recipe was a more exotic take on my childhood favorite & I was really curious as to how the flavors would marry. Crunchy, gooey, creamy, spicy, rich, decadent, savory, this sandwich conquers all of the grilled cheeses I have had & wins by a landslide. Thank you Matt's Kimchi for your amazing product so that I could create this delicious monster. You will love this, your kids will love this, if you like cheese, bread & crunch, go for it.

INGREDIENTS

2 Slices of Kalamata Olive Bread

Matt's Kimchi

3-4 Slices of Daiya Cheddar Cheese

1 Tbs Vegan Butter

1 Tbs Hampton Creek Just Mayo

INSTRUCTIONS

1. Heat up your skillet & add the butter.

2. While the butter is melting spread the mayo on the outsides of your slices of bread.

3. Place them, mayo side down, in the pan & allow them to crisp up.

4. As the bread begins to toast start piling on your cheese.

5. Let the cheese melt with the lid on for a few min. Add Matt's Kimchi & squish those bread slices together.

6. Place the lid back on & allow everything to finish cooking on low for a few more minutes.

7. Serve hot!

DILL RANCH & ROMAINE SALAD

Prep Time: 15 min | Total Time: 15 min | Serves: 1 Hungry Bunny

I have always had a thing for fresh dill. This powerful little herb seems to brighten up any dish & really add what seems like complex flavor. I had a lot of dill on hand one day & ended up with this recipe! Dill Ranch Dressing, filled with yummy creamy cashews, crisp cucumbers & lots of fresh herbs.

INGREDIENTS

2 Tbs of Dill Ranch Dressing

Romaine Lettuce

Kale

1 Tbs Hemp Seeds

Capers

Cucumbers

Edible Flowers for garnish

INSTRUCTIONS

1. Add the dressing to your salad & toss in a large bowl. If you'd like you can massage the dressing into the greens by hand.

2. Serve with additional Vinegar if you'd like more tang.

BANH MI

Prep Time: 5 min | Total Time: 5 min | Serves: 1 Hungry Bunny

My vegan rendition of the Banh Mi, worth the wait & the smell! I spent days studying the sandwiches components, understanding the flavors & concocting a recipe. The result was this, colorful, flavorful, palate defying sandwich! Thank you to my friend Joe for inspiring this recipe.

INGREDIENTS

Purple Cabbage

Rainbow Carrots

Radishes

Cucumber

Portebello Mushroom

Cilantro

1 Jalapeño

1 French baguette

Vegan mayo

Sriracha

Dill

½ C Vinegar

1-2 Tbs Maple Syrup

Pinch of Pink Himalayan salt Garlic

INSTRUCTIONS

1. Gather jars of choice, add thinly sliced veggies. I used veggies that I had readily available.

2. I separated my purple cabbage so that the color wouldn't spoil the other veggies coloring.

3. Add the vinegar, maple syrup & a pinch of salt to each jar & let them sit for 5 days in the fridge.

4. I grilled my portebello mushroom & lightly brushed it with coconut aminos & lime juice just to add a kick.

Side Note: Let me warn you about the smell because let me tell you, when you open up those radishes you will run the other way...I made this entire sandwich in my yard.

SIMPLE SUSHI

Prep Time: 15 min | Total Time: 15 min | Serves: 1 Hungry Bunny

This is probably my favorite go to lunch on a day that I don't want to make anything. The go to, an easy sushi roll that you can make without preparing rice, using fancy ingredients, or using a mat to roll them up. You can add whatever veggies you'd like to this & dip it into spicy mayo, coconut aminos, or peanut sauce.

INGREDIENTS

Nori

Kale Sprouts

Matt's Kimchi

Avocado

Coconut Aminos

INSTRUCTIONS

1. Take your sheet of nori & lay it onto a flat surface.

2. Take a fresh ripe avocado & spread it along the bottom of the nori.

3. Pile high with veggies of choice, I used Matt's Kimchi & kale sprouts.

4. Serve with coconut aminos.

*Side Note : Coconut Aminos can be purchased at health food stores. An alternative for this would be soy sauce.

ROMAINE, APPLE & FIG SUMMER SALAD

Prep Time: 5 min | Total Time: 5 min | Serves: 1 Hungry Bunny

---

This is such a refreshing & light salad with a smokey creamy dressing that catches you by surprise. When I have salads I need them to be savory & have lots of texture. This is a great dish to eat along side your dinner cr with your lunch. You can find the recipe for this dressing earlier on in this book, it was inspired by Kate Flowers. I love referencing her for raw salad dressings as well as other yummy desserts & smoothies!

INGREDIENTS

Romaine Lettuce

Green Apple

Yellow & Red Tomatoes

Cucumber

Figs

Sicilian Olives

Lime Juice

Strawberries

Pumpkin Seeds

Tahini Dressing

INSTRUCTIONS

1. Wash & prepare your lettuce or greens of choice & set aside.

2. Chop up all of your other fruits & veggies.

3. Top with fresh lime juice & tahini dressing.

RAINBOW WRAPS

I could seriously make sandwiches & wraps all day. There is sort of an art to it, the carefully paired ingredients, the colors, they're placement & all to create something that you can then eat!

INGREDIENTS

Sun dried Tomato Wrap

Spiraled Rainbow Carrots

Cucumber

Mashed Blueberries

Dill Sprouts

Roasted Brussels Sprouts

Yellow Tomatoes

Sriracha

Beets

Mustard Seed

INSTRUCTIONS

1. Grab your tortilla & Spread on some of the Sriracha.

2. Add on carrots, cucumber, blueberries, dill sprouts, roasted brussel sprouts, yellow tomatoes, beets & mustard seed.

3. Roll up carefully & enjoy.

NATURES CANDY BOWL

Prep Time: 15 min | Total Time: 15 min | Serves: 1-2 Hungry Bunny

---

If you have a sweet tooth like me & love your fruits then don't feel guilty about adding them to your salads! I find that this brightens up the salad & helps me feel more encouraged to eat more greens! I know this dish is rather simple, but I wanted to Share how beautiful and colorful you can make your salads. All you have to do is add fruits!

INGREDIENTS

Baby Kale

Spinach

Spring Mix

Cherry Tomatoes

Raspberries

Blackberries

Cucumber

Beets

Green Olives

Kiwi

INSTRUCTIONS

1. Fill your favorite bowl with all of the ingredients & top with your favorite dressing. I personally prefer balsamic & olive oil with this salad.

RAW BURRITOS

Prep Time: 20 min | Total Time: 20 min | Serves: 3-4 Hungry Bunnies

INGREDIENTS

1-2 C Walnuts

½-1 C Sun dried Tomatoes soaked 2+ Hours

1 tsp Chili Powder

½ tsp Cumin

½ tsp Smoked Paprika

½ tsp Whole Celery Seed

½ tsp Coriander

½ tsp Cayenne

½ tsp Pink Himalayan Salt

Cilantro to taste

1 Clove of Garlic

Avocado

Pico De Gallo + Purple Cabbage

Nacho Cheese

2 C Raw Cashews

½ C Nutritional Yeast

¼ C Water

¼ C Lemon Juice

¼ tsp Pink Himalayan Salt

2 Cloves Garlic

Sun Dried Tomato Jalapeño garlic spread

Raw Garlic, to taste (2-3 Cloves)

1 Lemon Juiced +Safflower oil for blending

1 Tbs Ground Flaxseed

Small Palm full of Sun Dried Tomato

1 Jalapeño

INSTRUCTIONS

1. Add walnuts, soaked sun dried tomatoes, chili powder, cumin, smoked paprika, celery seed, coriander, cayenne, salt, garlic, cilantro to your food processor & pulse until crumbly

2. In a Vitamix blender add 2 C raw cashews, nutritional yeast, water, lemon juice, salt, & garlic & blend until you get a creamy cheese, this will be the nacho cheese.

3. Grab a raw tortilla & spread on the nacho cheese, walnut meat, fresh pea sprouts, pico de gallo, purple cabbage, & garlic spread.

*Side Note: If you'd like you can wrap up your wrap with parchment paper prior to cutting it. This ensures that everything does not fall out. The sun-dried tomato jalapeño garlic spread was a pre-made spread. This can be substituted with any Miyoko's brand spread.

RAW ITALIAN WRAP

Prep Time: 10 min | Total Time: 10 min | Serves: 1 -2 Hungry Bunnies

INGREDIENTS

1 C Artichokes

1 Lemon Wedge

1 Tbs Italian Seasoning

1-2 Tbs Olive Oil

1 Tbs Raw Red Wine Vinegar

P nk Himalayan Salt to taste

DILL GARLIC SPREAD

Raw Garlic, to taste (2-3 Cloves)

1 Lemon Juiced +Safflower oil for blending

1 Tbs Ground Flaxseed

Sea Salt to taste

Fresh Dill to taste

TOPPINGS

Red Onion

Tomato

Pea Sprouts

Spiralized Sweet Potato

Kale

Purple Cabbage

Oil & Raw Red Wine Vinegar

INSTRUCTIONS

1. In a plastic bag add the artichokes,.emon, Italian seasoning, olive oil, vinegar, salt & allow all of the flavors to marinade overnight.

2. Take the raw garlic, lemon juice, flaxseed, salt, dill & blend it in a Vitamix blender.

3. Add some of the marinaded artichokes to your favorite tortilla.

4. Pile on some red onion, tomato, purple cabbage,pea sprouts, spiralized sweet potato, pea sprouts, kale.

5. Drizzle on some olive oil & vinegar before serving.

CHICKPEA & SPINACH SALAD

Prep Time: 10 min | Total Time: 10 min | Serves: 1-2 Hungry Bunnies

This chickpea salad is delicious on sandwiches, in salads, & even as a dip with fresh veggies. I personally could eat an entire serving of this myself. Adding chickpea salad in place of dressing really enhances the textures & flavors of the dish. Chickpeas are high in protein, fiber, vitamins & minerals & significantly boost your intake of manganese & folate. Chickpeas can add flavor & texture to a range of dishes & this is just one of them!

INGREDIENTS

1 C - 1 ½ C Chickpeas

3 Tbs Raw Vegan Mayo

½-1 Tbs Fresh Dill

1 Tbs Pickle Juice

Salt & Pepper to taste

½ a pound of Spinach

Carrots

RAW VEGAN MAYO

¼ C Water

¼ C Olive Oil

1 C Cashews

3 Tbs Lemon Juice

1 ¼ tsp Mustard Powder

1 tsp Apple Cider Vinegar

¼ tsp Salt

⅓ C Sunflower Seeds

INSTRUCTIONS

1. Add your chickpeas, vegan mayo, fresh dill, pickle juice, salt & pepper to your food processor.

2. Pulse until slightly crumbly but not pureed.

3. Taste & see if anything else is needed.

4. Toss into a salad & enjoy!

SAVORY

PUMPKIN SAGE PASTA

Prep Time: 15 min | Total Time: 30-35 min | Serves: 4-6 Hungry Bunnies

I would imagine eating this dish in the fall, while basking in the warm sun on a cool day. With each bite I would find myself admiring all of the foliage while planning to pick pine cones & collect leaves to press. My favorite thing to do in the fall was collect leaves that I would press in textbooks with my mother. It was a tradition & I still do it to this day.

This recipe was inspired by Sophie Uliano, I explored by adding some of my own personal touches but this recipe is so simple & beautiful. If you are not familiar with using black bean noodles then you may also use regular pasta or zucchini noodles. I personally love black bean noodles because they have so much nutritional value as well as lots of protein!

INGREDIENTS

1 tsp Coconut Oil

½ of a Yellow Onion

1 Shallot

4 Cloves of Garlic

1 tsp White Pepper

½ of 1 can of Pumpkin Puree

½ C cooked Sweet Potato

Handful of Sun Dried Tomatoes

2 tsp of Cayenne Pepper

1 C Nut Milk

3-4 Fresh Sage Leaves

Black Bean Spaghetti

INSTRUCTIONS

1. Sauté onions & garlic in the coconut oil until softened & fragrant.

2. Add to a blender & puree with pumpkin, sweet potato & all of the other ingredients.

3. Bring a pot of water to a boil & add in your pasta.

4. Once your pasta is finished cooking drain the water & add in the sauce.

5. Stir in sauce until it heats up & you are ready to go!

6. Garnish with sage & sun dried tomatoes & prepare to fall in love.

THE BIG MAC

Prep Time: 5 min | Total Time: 10 min | Serves: 1 Hungry Bunny

Who needs beef patties when you could have an entirely plant based burger that will fill you up, satisfy all of your hopes & dreams while being healthy?! My ultimate weakness has always been a good burger. I used to always order a California burger because I loved the "special sauce." (Which we all know is thousand island dressing) This burger is smokey, crispy, savory, mouthwatering & a huge favorite in my home. Throw this on a grill at a family BBQ with a couple slices of daiya cheese & you will fool any meat lover. I know I did not actually make this burger but this "recipe" is in here to share a staple I go to. This is something I eat when I don't feel like cooking as well as my favorite way to prepare it!

INGREDIENTS

1 Beyond Meat Burger Patty

1 Tbs Olive Oil or Butter

2 Slices of Daiya Cheese

2 Tbs of "special sauce"

Tomato

Onion

Lettuce

Salt

Pepper

Ketchup

Seeded Bun or Bun of choice

Dill Pickles

INSTRUCTIONS

1. If you are using a grill for this recipe then go ahead & start heating that up. If you are using a skillet then begin heating that up as well with a Tbs of butter or oil.

2. When the grill or pan is hot then you can go ahead & add your burgers. Let them crisp up on eat side, this should be quite fast, 5-7 minutes.

3. Once you have cooked your burger almost fully add on two slices of Daiya cheese & place a lid over it so that the cheese melts. In the meantime prep your "special sauce."

4. The "special sauce" is essentially thousand island dressing, you can use your own recipe of the one I provide in this book. Toast your buns & spread on the sauce.

5. Add some lettuce, a burger, tomato, onions, pickles & more sauce. Enjoy!

RAINBOW PINWHEELS

Prep Time: 10 min | Total Time: 15-20 min | Serves: 3-4 Hungry Bunnies

Rainbow Swiss Chard may very well be the prettiest leafy green in all of the land. My family & I usually make spinach pinwheel bread.

This is a dish that I always look forward to & could probably add to the list of "things I'd eat everyday." However, with some beautiful sweet greens like these I thought it would be a nice change to prepare the bread with chard instead. I love how vibrant the colors are in this bread & the raisins really bring out the sweetness in the greens. You may also add pignoli nuts to this for a bit of a crunch!

INGREDIENTS

1 Bushel of Rainbow Swiss Chard

½ C Raisins or Currants

¼-½ C Vegetable Broth

2-5 Cloves of Garlic (you guys are on your own for this one because I LOVE my garlic)

Fresh Pizza Dough

Pignoli Nuts

INSTRUCTIONS

1. Thoroughly wash the greens & cut into 1"-2" pieces, I generally just give them a rough chop.

2. Sauté in garlic & vegetable broth until softened, if you'd like you could add the raisins here so they absorb all of the juices & flavors.

3. Spread the dough out so it covers a rectangular cookie sheet, then pour in the greens & spread out evenly.

4. Begin to carefully roll up the bread. Add some parchment paper to your cookie sheet & place on the grill for 30 minutes.

5. Be sure to watch it & possibly flip it to ensure that it does not burn. Slice, admire the colors, & devour.

BROCCOLI RABE SANDWICH

Prep Time: 10 min | Total Time: 20-30 min | Serves: 2-3 Hungry Bunnies

Broccoli rabe is always a staple in my home. My family eats it at least once a week & I definitely have continued the tradition on my own.

One day I decided to throw it onto a grilled cheese & from that day forward I never looked at broccoli rabe the same. This is a great green to add to sandwiches, eat with pasta dishes & even over creamy mashed potatoes. I hope you guys love the combination as much as I do!

INGREDIENTS

1-2 Bushels of Broccoli Rabe

6-8 Cloves of Garlic

Chao Creamy Original Cheese

2 Tbs Olive Oil

Crushes Red Pepper to taste

Salt & Black Pepper to taste

Sliced Bread of choice

Sauerkraut

Spicy Brown Mustard

INSTRUCTIONS

1. Start by bringing a large pot of salted water to a boil.

2. Cut an X in the bottom of the stems of the broccoli rabe & place in the boiling water.

3. In a large heavy skillet over medium heat. Heat olive oil & sauté garlic for 1 to 2 minutes.

4. Stir in the broccoli rabe & sauté 10 to 15 minutes. Remove from skillet & set aside.

5. Take 2 Slices of slice bread or bread of choice & spread on some spicy brown mustard, place into the same skillet. Top with a few slices of Chao, creamy original, cheese.

6. Let the bread toast in the pan until the cheese melts & the bread turns crispy & golden.

7. Once the cheese is gooey & melted begin adding on the sautéed broccoli rabe, some salt, pepper to taste & if you'd like crushed red pepper.

8. Top with sauerkraut & place the slices together

GRILLED EGGPLANT

Prep Time: 5 min | Total Time: 35 min | Serves: Servings Vary

This is a holiday favorite in my family & has been for many years. Every time there is any form of celebration this dish is sure to be present. My personal favorite component of this dish is the fact that it only gets better with each day. The longer the ingredients get to sit together the more the flavors marry & soak into the eggplant. This is a great dish to add to an antipasti, eat alone, or pile high onto sandwiches.

INGREDIENTS

2 Large Eggplant

½ - 1C of Fresh Picked Mint from my garden

6+ Cloves of Garlic

Olive Oil

Balsamic Vinegar to taste

*Side Note: Add Balsamic according to how sweet you want this dish to be, start off light, you can always add more later on. Also I personally prefer the eggplant to be so thin that you can see through it, however, if you are unable to do this than that is fine the eggplant will just take some more time to cook.

INSTRUCTIONS

1. Begin by allowing your grill pan to get very hot, this is the type of dish where you have to work as you prep in order to prevent the eggplant from turning color.

2. Wash, peel & slice your eggplant as thin as you possibly can, the thinner the better. Immediately begin adding the sliced eggplant to the grill pan & let it cook until its almost completely finished, depending on the thickness this could range between 5-10 minutes.

3. In the meantime pour some olive oil into a deep serving dish, sprinkle in some of the chopped garlic. Return to your grill pan & make sure the eggplant is cooking properly, it is okay if it burns a bit.

4. Once the first round of eggplant is finished grilling immediately add it to your serving dish, drizzle with more olive oil, more chopped garlic, fresh mint & a splash of balsamic. Continue this process, layering until your serving dish is piled high & full.

SUN DRIED TOMATO PASTA

Prep Time: 10 min | Total Time: 10 min | Serves: 3-4 Hungry Bunnies

The best kind of pasta is the one that really grabs all the good stuff in your dish. I love making pastas, like rigatoni, that seem to scoop up all of the beans, spinach, the juices & the sauce. It makes every bite filled with flavor & really hearty. I usually make this dish on the nights I don't want to cook. I came up with it on a night that I got home, with limited drive to cook & limited ingredients. You could easily throw this together in the amount of time the pasta takes to cook.

INGREDIENTS

Pasta of choice

6 Sun Dried Tomatoes, soaked in Olive Oil + 2 Tbs of the Olive Oil

Small Palm full of Fresh Parsley

3-6 Cloves of Garlic

1 Tbs Nutritional Yeast (optional)

½ of 1 Yellow Onion

1 Tbs of Balsamic (optional)

1 16 oz can of Cannellini Beans

2 Sprigs of Fresh Basil

Pink Himalayan Salt & Pepper to taste

3 C of Fresh Spinach

INSTRUCTIONS

1. Bring a pot of salted water to a boil. Add in your pasta & allow it to cook.

2. Heat up a pan with the two Tbs of olive oil from the sun dried tomatoes, garlic, onion, salt & pepper. Sauté until golden brown, add a splash of balsamic.

3. Add in your sun dried tomatoes & cannellini beans. Begin to crush them with a fork. Add in 2 Tbs of the water from the pasta, add in the spinach & basil & place a lid on top.

4. Once the spinach is wilted add your nutritional yeast, salt & pepper to taste. Add some fresh parsley & the cooked pasta.

5. Mix thoroughly & serve with fresh parsley.

CHIPOTLE TAQUITOS

I love snack foods & hand held foods, who doesn't love eating with their hands? This is such a special, spicy, flavorful & delicious dish that is a unique addition to any taco Tuesday or appetizer spread. I love drizzling these with fresh lime juice & hot sauce & serving them with salsa, queso or guacamole. Don't forget, chipotle has a bit of a kick to it & if you are not someone who enjoys spicy foods then I suggest being more cautious with the adobo sauce. You could even substitute for some mild salsa & chipotle hot sauce or liquid smoke.

INGREDIENTS

½ of an Onion

1 Tbs Olive Oil + more for drizzling

1 Garlic Clove

1 Can of Black Beans

1 Tbs Chili Powder

1 Tbs Cumin

1 Tbs Chipotle Adobo Sauce + 1 Chipotle Pepper

Salt & Pepper to taste

Corn Tortilla's

1 Tbs Fresh Lime juice

INSTRUCTIONS

1. Preheat your oven to 350°

2. Heat up a pan with the one Tbs of olive oil. Add your garlic & onion & sauté until golden.

3. Add chili powder, cumin, salt & pepper to taste. Taste & adjust seasoning then add the adobo sauce plus the chipotle pepper & mix to incorporate.

4. Finally add in your black beans along with some fresh lime juice. Mix & mash the beans with your fork, be sure to leave some texture. Remove the mixture from the gas & set aside.

5. Start grabbing your tortilla's & place them in the hot oven. Let them soften & then immediately remove them & add 1 Tbs of filling.

6. Carefully roll, place on a greased baking sheet & brush with olive oil. Bake for 20 min then raise the temperature to 400° & let them crisp up for 10 min.

CREAMY KELP NOODLES

Creamy Kelp Noodles will prove that you can still enjoy noodles or pasta while eating a raw diet. I love these noodles for a summer dish, they are super refreshing & light but also impressively satisfying. You could bring this dish to a summer BBQ & share some healthy noodles with your friends & family. I loved eating this with Matt's Kimchi on top, it really added some flavor & tang to the dish.

INGREDIENTS

¼-½ C Creamy Asian Dressing

1 Package of Kelp Noodles (Soaked overnight)

Matt's Kimchi

Black Sesame Seeds

Shitake Mushrooms

Fresh Cabbage

Lemon

INSTRUCTIONS

1. About 1 hour before creating this dish soak your kelp noodles one last time with one fresh lemon.

2. Rinse & drain your noodles.

3. Pour on some of the creamy Asian dressing & toss thoroughly.

4. Top with Matt's Kimchi, fresh cabbage, sesame seeds, mushrooms & whatever other veggies you'd like.

*Side Note : Kelp Noodles can be purchased at health food stores. An alternative for this would any other noodles of choice. The kelp noodles are what keep this dish raw.

BEEF & BROCCOLI *Natasha Najjar*

Prep Time: 10 min | Total Time: Overnight | Serves: 2-3 Hungry Bunnies

INGREDIENTS

2 14oz cans Jackfruit

4 tsp Tamari

1 tsp Apple Cider Vinegar

2 ½ C or 1 lb dry short grain Brown Rice

8 Cloves Garlic

1 medium sized Shallot

½ Lime

2 tsp Black strap Molasses

4 tsp Maple Syrup

1 Tbs Apple Cider Vinegar

2 Tbs Cornstarch

2 Large bunches of Broccoli

4 Tbsp of Avocado Oil

Sesame Seeds for garnishing

*Side Note : Apple Cider Vinegar can be purchased at any major super market chain as well as health food stores.

INSTRUCTIONS

1. Open the cans of jackfruit & over a colander, use your fist to press the fruit into the colander squeezing every last bit of water out.

2. In a small bowl mix the fruit with the tamari & apple cider vinegar let this sit, then begin preparing your brown rice.

3. Mince shallot & garlic into tiny pieces. Place garlic, shallot & lime juice in a bowl & set aside.

4. Whisk the liquid ingredients in a small bowl & slowly add all of the cornstarch. This will be the main savory sauce to cover the "beef" in. After 5 minutes or more the sauce will thicken.

5. Cut the broccoli into medium & small sized pieces. Heat 2 tsp of the avocado oil & add them to a non stick wok or pan. Add ⅓ C water & cover to steam for 2 minutes.

6. Add in the marinated jackfruit with 2 Tbsp of the oil & cook on medium heat for 10 minutes stirring constantly.

7. Add the garlic, shallot & lime & cook for 2 more minutes. Finally add the thickened sauce, giving it a quick whisk once more, & cook for about 5 to 7 minutes.

8. Stir in broccoli & cook until its a little brown & crispy on the outside. Serve the with brown rice.

BBQ JACKFRUIT SANDWICH

Prep Time: 15 min | Total Time: 30 min | Serves: 3-4 Hungry Bunnies

INGREDIENTS

2 20 oz cans Young Green Jack-fruit in water

1 bottle of BBQ sauce

2 Tbsp Coconut Sugar

1 tsp Paprika

2 tsp Garlic Powder

1 tsp Onion Powder

½ tsp Cayenne Pepper

½ tsp Pepper

½ tsp Chili Powder

1 tsp Cajun seasoning

TOPPINGS

Cole Slaw

Hampton Creek Just Mayo

Kale

Red Onion

Ezekiel Bread

Pickles

Mango

INSTRUCTIONS

1. Begin by straining & thoroughly drying the canned jack-fruit.

2. Check for tough bits of the jack-fruit or the "core" & discard, place the remaining pieces in a bowl & begin mixing in your seasoning.

3. Heat a large skillet over medium heat & add 1-2 Tbsp of olive oil, once the pan is hot begin adding in the seasoned jackfruit.

4. Cook for 2-3 minutes while gently tossing the jack-fruit to ensure that it does not burn. You can now add the BBQ sauce & reduce the heat to low- medium.

5. Cook for 30 minutes in order to achieve a "slow cooked" flavor, if need be reduce the temperature to prevent burning.

6. Remove lid & stir occasionally. For a little extra color turn up the temperature at the very end! This gives the jack-fruit some more character & texture! Serve with Cole Slaw on a bun with a little more BBQ sauce & enjoy!

PENNE VODKA

Prep Time: 15 min | Total Time: 2-3 hours | Serves: 2-3 Hungry Bunnies

Penne vodka is the ultimate comfort food & when I worked at a pizzeria I used to get this any chance I got & I loved every second of it. As soon as I changed my eating habits I needed to fill the hole in my heart for this dish, & here it is.

INGREDIENTS

24 oz Can of Whole San Marzano Tomatoes (pureed)

3-6 Cloves of Garlic (I'm a Garlic Nut)

½ of an Onion

1-2 Tbs Olive oil

Salt & Pepper to taste

2 Bay Leafs

Small Palm full of Fresh Basil

1 Tbs Crushed Red Pepper (or to taste)

2-3 Tbs Cashew Ricotta Cheese + 1 Shot of Vodka (optional)

Capers

Eggplant Meatballs

Pasta of choice

Extra Olive Oil for drizzling

INSTRUCTIONS

1. Heat your oil until it is hot. Add in the onion, garlic, salt & pepper to taste.

2. Once the garlic is nice & browned & the onions have caramelized a bit carefully begin to pour in your pureed tomatoes. You want to be careful that the liquid does not shoot back at you.

3. Toss in some fresh basil & a bay leaf

4. Allow the sauce to come to a bowl, with the lid on. Then reduce to a simmer & slightly slant the lid.

5. Let the sauce cook for a few hours, stirring occasionally.

6. Bring a pot of salted water to a boil.

7. Add in your pasta & allow it to cook.

8. While the pasta is cooking return to your sauce. Add in 1 shot of vodka, & 2-3 Tbs of the cream sauce. Let the alcohol cook for about 5 minutes.

9. Add your pasta with 1-2 Tbs of the water to the sauce & serve with capers.

*Side Note: Cashew Ricotta Cheese recipe is featured on my website. You can also sub for Kite Hill Ricotta Cheese. This recipe is featured in HOC Supper Club Magazines summer addition.

EGGPLANT MEATBALLS

I use this recipe for the meatballs featured with my Penne Vodka recipe. These meatballs are addicting, I promise you will be picking them off the pan but be careful not to burn your fingers! These are great for Sunday pasta, I always recommend doubling this batch!

INGREDIENTS

1 Medium Eggplant

3-6 Cloves of Garlic

½ of an Onion

¼ C Raisins

1-1 ½ Tbs Olive Oil + 1 Tbs (for drizzling)

¾ C GF Breadcrumbs

½ tsp Oregano

½ C Carrot

1 Tbs Balsamic (optional)

Small Palm full of fresh Parsley

¼ C Pignoli Nuts (optional)

Salt & Pepper to taste

INSTRUCTIONS

1. Preheat your oven to 400° degrees.

2. Peel & chop up your eggplant, onion, garlic, & carrots.

3. Put them on a cookie sheet & drizzle on some olive oil, oregano salt & pepper.

4. Place them in the oven & allow them to roast for 30 minutes, tossing & adding balsamic about halfway through.

5. When 30 minutes hits decrease your oven to 350° &,depending on if you need to, let them roast for 10 more minutes.

6. Remove from the oven & add to a food processor.

7. Add the bread crumbs, & parsley. Pulse until the mixture is combined & mailable.

8. Remove the mixture & add to a bowl. Add in your raisins & mix with your hands.

9. Form small meatballs (Tbs size) & place them back onto the cookie sheet.

10. If you need to, add more olive oil to prevent the meatballs from sticking & place them into the oven to cook for 30 minutes so they crisp up.

TRUFFLE PIE

Prep Time: 10 min | Total Time: 20-30 min | Serves: 4-6 Hungry Bunnies

Truffle is a beautiful & special ingredient that I sometimes add to my dishes. It is not that often, but when I decide to be extra fancy I always resort to truffles. These pizzas are great to make on a hot summer evening. Have you ever cooked a pie on the grill? They come out with a totally different taste & texture & make for a great way to avoid using the oven on a hot day. I love the combination of the earthy arugula & truffle, this is a great appetizer or entrée for any event.

INGREDIENTS

Fresh Pizza Dough
(purchased from a local pizzeria)

Fresh Arugula

Cyster Mushrooms

Truffle Oil

Fresh Rosemary

Clive Oil for drizzling

Roasted Garlic

INSTRUCTIONS

1. Lightly drizzle some olive oil onto your cookie sheet.

2. Spread out your pizza dough onto a pizza stone or cookie sheet.

3. Brush Truffle oil over your pizza dough along with some fresh rosemary & place the pizza dough onto your grill.

4. Let the dough fluff up & start to get golden (underneath)

5. Once the dough starts to get golden underneath remove the dough from the grill & set aside.

6. Heat up a cast iron skillet & add in your mushrooms with a little splash of truffle oil.

7. Sauté until soft & tender.

8. Grab your roasted garlic & smash it up into a paste.

9. Spread the paste onto your pizza dough & add on your mushrooms.

10. If you'd like the dough to be crisper you can place it back onto the grill for a bit. Top with fresh arugula & serve.

BURRITO BOWL

Prep Time: 15 min | Total Time: 50 min | Serves: 2 Hungry Bunnies

---

Going to chipotle is always a good time, you get your delicious burrito, or burrito bowl, if your like me then you always opt for guacamole & you leave totally & completely satisfied. I used to go very often, but my wallet was not very happy about it so I decided to make an easy & lazy option for those nights I want take out without spending the money! However, I am guilty & will admit that I was so busy creating this dish that I forgot the guacamole, who does that?! Please feel free to add some to this dish, I know I would!

INGREDIENTS

1 C White Rice

4 C Spinach

1 Tbs Olive Oil

2-3 Tbs Chipotle Mayo

1 Can of Pinto Beans

1 Small Head of Broccoli

Tomato

Kale Sprouts

Jalapeño

Avocado

Salt & Pepper to taste

Salsa (optional)

Hot Sauce (optional)

INSTRUCTIONS

1. Start by adding your rice to your rice cooker. Cook for about 30 minutes.

2. While the rice is cooking you can begin steaming your broccoli & sautéing the spinach.

3. Add 1 Tbs of olive oil to your skillet & allow it to heat up. Add your freshly washed spinach & let it wilt down while stirring frequently. Remove from pan & set aside.

4. Rinse & strain your pinto beans & add them to the same pan. Sauté in the remaining oils to heat them up. If you'd like you could add chipotle flakes while cooking, as well as salt & pepper to taste

5. Once the rice has finished you may start building your bowl. If you'd like the base could be mostly spinach (raw or sautéed) I personally used rice.

6. Add all of your toppings & enjoy!

KIMCHI REUBEN

Prep Time: 10 min | Total Time: 15 min | Serves: 2 Hungry Bunnies

Caramelizing onions & mushrooms properly really brings out a deep savory flavor which really makes this sandwich. I am super picky when it comes to my sandwiches & I consider each one I make a masterpiece.

This beautiful & palate defying sandwich really impressed me. I loved the combination of the Russian dressing, sauerkraut & kimchi. Grilling the bread for this sandwich really takes it to the next level. If you'd like to really crank it up a notch then you may spread some olive oil & crushed garlic on each side of the bread prior to grilling.

INGREDIENTS

2 Portebello Mushrooms

½ Large White Onion

1 Tbs Dill

1 Tbs Olive Oil

1 Tbs Pickle juice

Rye Sourdough Bread

Cashew Scallion Nut Cheese

Russian Dressing

Sauerkraut

Persian Cucumber (thinly sliced)

Matt's Kimchi

Kale Sprouts (optional)

INSTRUCTIONS

1. Start by heating up the olive oil & the pickle juice until the oil is simmering.

2. Add the onions & the mushrooms & sauté for 3-5 minutes stirring occasionally & adding more pickle juice if need be.

3. Set the sautéed veggies aside & begin grilling your bread. Once the bread is grilled generously spread the cashew scallion nut cheese on both sides.

4. At this point you can add on the cucumber slices, the mushrooms & onions, Matt's Kimchi, sauerkraut, & thousand island dressing.

*Side Note: Russian dressing & Thousand Island dressing are often confused. They both have mayonnaise & ketchup as a base, but where Thousand Island is a bit sweet containing relish, Russian dressing has more of a kick, with a hint of heat from horseradish. This however, is my own personal take on it!

AVOCADO FIESTA BURGER

Prep Time: 10 min | Total Time: 15-20 min | Serves: 1 Hungry Bunny

If you are like me then you know that avocado is good with pretty much everything. You live for it, eat it daily & never think twice about paying extra for it at Chipotle. That is why if you are like me you need this raw vegan avocado fiesta burger in your life.

No, avocado may not be the most practical vessel to hold your burger & toppings, yes, it may be messy, but it is delicious! This is a great way to substitute bread & add some creamy goodness to your meal. Be prepared to get your hands dirty & dig in!

INGREDIENTS

Shaved Carrots

¼ tsp Pink Himalayan Salt

Purple Potato

Sweet Peas

Tomato

Kale

Dill Ranch Dressing

Herb Cream Cheese

Raw Fiesta Burger

1 Perfectly Ripe Avocado

INSTRUCTIONS

1. Take your ripe avocado & carefully peel the skin off. Cut in half & remove the pit, set aside.

2. Smother on some of the dill ranch cream cheese

3. Slice your potatoes super thin & place in a small bowl with some salt & olive oil. Then begin piling on your other ingredients.

4. Start by piling on the cucumbers, carrots & some dill ranch dressing.

5. Add on your burger & whatever other toppings you'd like!

Side Note: To ensure that the skin comes off of your avocado perfectly be sure to use one that is ripe but not over ripe. Carefully pull back the skin & peel it carefully until you have removed all of it. The recipe for the Raw Fiesta burger will be featured on my website.

THE GARDEN SUB

Prep Time: 10 min | Total Time: 10 min | Serves: 1-2 Hungry Bunnies

I always loved watching my dad make subs. He had such precision, so much focus, & always seasoned everything perfectly. I like to think I took after him when it comes to my dedication to sandwich making & as you guys know by now I love my sandwiches.

This is a fusion between an Italian sub & a grilled veggies sub. I love using my grilled eggplant for this recipe as well as some fresh tomatoes, oil & vinegar & arugula.

INGREDIENTS

2 Tbs Pesto

¼ C Vegan Mayo

Oil & red vinegar

Tomato

Grilled Eggplant

Arugula & Baby Kale

Sprouts

Red Onion

Grilled Red Cabbage

PESTO

1/2 C steamed peas

2 C spinach

2 sprigs of fresh oregano

½ C fresh basil

½ C fresh parsley

2 cloves of fresh garlic

INSTRUCTIONS

1. Slice your roll & place it face down on the grill so it gets a light char.

2. Remove & spread on some pesto mayo, this is simply a palm full of fresh basil, a palm full of arugula & 3-5 green olives blended with mayo.

3. Top with your veggies, I used the grilled eggplant, arugula, baby kale, sprouts, red onion, grilled cabbage, tomato oil & vinegar.

4. Serve with roasted potatoes.

THE PHILLY BOY

Prep Time: 20 min | Total Time: 30 min | Serves: 2-3 Hungry Bunnies

I will never forget the first time I had a Philly cheese steak, in fact my mouth is watering as I'm writing this recipe. No matter what my lifestyle is, there will never be anything that beats a good sandwich & this one took my heart by a storm.

Supposedly a good cheese steak is all about the bread, lots of ketchup & super melty cheese. However, I have never heard much talk about the steak so why not keep all the best parts while enhancing this sandwich even more? Here is a great hearty dinner that is built to satisfy.

INGREDIENTS

1 Tbs Olive Oil

1 Yellow Onion (Large)

3 Bell Peppers

24 oz of Mushrooms

1 Tbs Cajun Creole Seasoning

1-2 C Daiya Cheddar Cheese

1 French Baguette

Vegan Mayo

Ketchup

INSTRUCTIONS

1. Add the olive oil to a skillet & let it warm up, then add in your onions.

2. Let the onions cook until they begin to smell fragrant & become more transparent.

3. Add in the bell peppers, mushrooms & creole seasoning. Allow everything to cook on high for 15 minutes.

4. Add The Daiya Cheddar Cheese, remove the pan from the gas & allow the cheese to melt.

5. Take your bread of choice & spread your favorite vegan mayo onto one side, spread ketchup on the other side. Add your filling & serve with ketchup!

CAJUN CREOLE SLIDERS

Prep Time: 1 hr 15 min | Total Time: 1 hour 20 min | Serves: 5-6 Hungry Bunnies

Plant based burgers are their own mystery. You can either have a great one or an okay one & I am here to provide you guys with a recipe for one that is guaranteed to be delicious! Burgers were always my favorite so when it came time to create a healthy plant based one I was, without a doubt, ready to satisfy all of the expectations of the traditional burger! Crispy, savory, hearty & comforting this is a dinner that is perfect to make at a BBQ & is meant to be savored.

INGREDIENTS

1 Can of Tri Bean Blend (Black Beans, Kidney Beans, Pinto Beans)

½ of One White Onion

4 Shitake Mushrooms

1 Tbs Olive Oil

1-2 Tbs Worcestershire Sauce

½ C Walnuts

¾ C GF Oats

1 Tbs Cajun Creole Spice

1 Tbs Capers + 1 Tbs Juice

1 tsp Rosemary

1 Garlic Clove (optional)

Russian Dressing

Matt's Kimchi

Kale Sprouts

Smokey Cashew Cheese

Tomato

INSTRUCTIONS

1. Add 1 Tbs of olive oil to a skillet & let it warm up, then add in your onions.

2. Let the onions cook until they begin to smell fragrant & become more transparent then add the mushrooms. Then transfer to a bowl & set aside

3. In a food processor add the walnuts, Oats, Spices & pulse twice, then add in the sautéed onions & mushrooms, the beans, Worcestershire sauce, capers with their juice & pulse until crumbly. Place in the refrigerator for 1 hour.

4. Remove from the fridge & form patties, add them to a hot skillet & let them crisp up on each side.

5. Transfer to a cookie sheet & bake at 350° for 30 minutes, flipping them halfway through. Crank the oven to 400° & let them finish cooking for 15 minutes.

6. Assemble burgers & enjoy!

ESCAROLE & BEANS

Prep Time: 15-20 min | Total Time: 1 hr 30 min | Serves: 3-4 Hungry Bunnies

Escarole & beans is a dish that goes back with me to my childhood.

This traditional dish gives you that warm & cozy feeling of a good hearty meal but without the guilt. The earthy escarole has sturdy leaves & a mild, bitter flavor. It's a great green for soups & stews & side dishes. For this recipe we pair it with cannellini beans to compliment the greens & supply a nutty earthy flavor to the dish.

INGREDIENTS

2 Heads of Escarole

1 whole bag of Cannellini soaked overnight & cooked for an 1 & 30 minutes

Garlic, by preference, I use 5 cloves

Splash of White Wine

4 C of Vegetable Broth

Crushed Red Pepper

INSTRUCTIONS

1. Sauté garlic & a little bit of olive oil until fragrant & then add your *thoroughly* washed escarole.

2. Add your vegetable broth & let the greens cook down for about one hour.

3. Then you want to add your beans, crushed red pepper & the white wine & let everything cook together for about 30 minutes.

4. The final result is so lovely, the beans create a slight thickness to the broth & all the flavors truly come together beautifully.

*Side Note: I stress thoroughly because escarole has a lot of grit & sand & you want to be sure to get all that out!

SUN DRIED TOMATO & WHITE BEAN ALFREDO *Michelle Gerrard-Marriott*

Prep Time: 15-20 min | Total Time: 1 hr 45 min | Serves: 4-6 Hungry Bunnies

This is a warm, vibrant & sensational dish that I approve of to the moon & back. Here is a recipe from The Vibrant Kitchen & home, an elegant step back to nature.

INGREDIENTS

1 16oz GF Spaghetti

6 oz Sun Dried Tomatoes in Olive Oil

2 bunches Parsley

1 bunch Basil

29 oz Cannellini Beans

3 Lemons

6 Cloves of Garlic minced

One Sweet Onion

5 Roma Tomatoes sliced & then halved

1 tsp Red Pepper

1 pint Cherry Tomatoes (for roasting)

1 Red Pepper (for roasting)

1 full bulb of Garlic (for roasting)

2-3 Tbs Dark Chocolate Balsamic Vinegar (or any balsamic you have on hand)

INSTRUCTIONS

1. Preheat oven to 350°.

2. Place the red pepper on a cookie sheet & rub a small amount of olive oil all over. Lightly dust with salt & pepper and set aside.

3. Add your tomatoes to the roasting dish. Splash on about two Tbs of olive oil. Follow with a Tbs or so of dark chocolate balsamic vinegar.

4. Chop about ¼ of the top of the bulb of garlic off & then wrap full bulb in aluminum foil. Place in the oven & let them roast for about an hour & 15 min to an hour & 30 min.

5. Start boiling water for your pasta. Add salt & a small splash of olive oil.

6. Heat a saucepan with olive oil & add garlic & onion with a tiny bit of salt & pepper. Allow to become fragrant & add a bit of your basil & parsley as well as your sun dried & Roma tomatoes.

7. Strain your Cannellini beans & add to a food processor along with zest of one lemon, salt, pepper, basil, parsley, juice of two lemons, roasted garlic, & red pepper.

8. Process until smooth. Add Cannellini mixture ½ cup at a time into your saucepan & mix until combined.

9. Start by adding the ½ cup, if you want a creamier texture you can add more in small batches until you reach the consistency you desire.

10. Cook your pasta in the boiling water, strain when done & add into saucepan. Top with roasted tomatoes, roasted red pepper fresh squeezed lemon juice & freshly ground pepper. Enjoy!

HEART OF THE SEA *Michelle Gerrard-Marriott*

Prep Time: 20 min | Total Time: 45 min-1 hr | Serves: 8-10 Hungry Bunnies

---

These patties are such a nice summer dish. They can be eaten as is, cn top of a bed of greens, mashed potatoes or on a fresh roll of bread. They are crispy, flavorful & have beautiful texture.

If you are cutting back on oil, these are just as delicious shallow fried with just a Tbs of oil!

INGREDIENTS

2 Jars Hearts of Palm

2 Ears of Fresh Corn, or Frozen

1 Bunch of Green Oniors

1 Large Red Bell Pepper

2 Bunches of Cilantro

1 Bunch Italian Parsley

4 Cloves of Minced Garlic

3 Roasted Carrots

Zest of 1 Lemon

Juice of 2 Lemons

½ tsp Paprika

1 ½ tsp Sumac

2 C GF Vegan Panko Bread Crumbs + 2 more C for coating

3 Tbs Vegan Mayo

Pink salt & pepper to taste

Coconut oil for frying

THOUSAND ISLAND SAUCE

½ Vegan Mayo

2 Tbs Ketchup

1-2 tsp Sriracha

Juice of one Lemon

HEART OF THE SEA *Michelle Gerrard-Marriott* **CONTINUED**

INSTRUCTIONS

1. Preheat oven to 375° First off prep all of your veggies & herbs.

2. Drain your corn. Wash & chop your green onions, cilantro, parsley, bell pepper & garlic.

3. Wash your carrots & then put them in a roasting dish with some olive oil salt & pepper. Pop in the oven & roast for 35-40 minutes until gently browned & tender.

4. Drain your hearts of palm & put them in a food processor. Gently pulse until flakes form. You want it to be flaky but not mushy. If there are larger chunks left that is OK they add great texture!

5. Add your flaked hearts of palm to a large bowl. Now add your chopped cilantro, bell pepper, green onions, cilantro, parsley, garlic, corn, lemon zest & juice, 2 cups of breadcrumbs, veganaise, paprika, sumac, pink salt & pepper. Mix well with your hands.

6. Set out some parchment paper & sprinkle bread crumbs on paper. Begin forming your patties & laying them on the parchment. I made larger servings of patties & made 13 in total.

7. Grab patties individually & coat with bread crumbs. Put them back on the parchment.

8. Prep a deep cast iron pan on medium heat. Add about ½ cup of coconut oil.

9. When oil is melted, place your patties in the pan. You want to hear a gentle sizzle that is when you know the pan is at the right temperature.

10. Fry patties on each side for 4-5 minutes until golden brown!

11. When all your patties are fried you can top them with thousand island & fresh squeezed lemon juice.

A BITE OF BLISS
POTATO TACOS *Michelle Gerrard-Marriott*

Prep Time: 15-20 min | Total Time: 1 hr 30 min | Serves: 3-4 Hungry Bunnies

Organic Sprouted Corn Tortillas hold so much bounty. Yukon Golden potatoes spiced to perfection & roasted until crispy. Seasonal Squash, sweet onions, & garlic roasted until fragrant & gorgeous. Red bell pepper for a burst of flavor & vitamin c & cilantro really brighten this dish & tie it together.

INGREDIENTS

6-7 Yukon Gold Potatoes cut into small cubes

2 Zucchini or any seasonal squash chopped into small cubes

1 red onion cut into quarters

1 sweet onion cut into quarters

6 cloves of garlic minced

1 bunch of cilantro

1 bunch of chives

1 head of romaine lettuce

2- 3 tsp turmeric

2-3 tsp smoked paprika

2-3 tsp cumin

1 tsp black pepper

½ tsp cayenne

2 tsp of pink salt or more depending on taste

Organic Sprouted Corn Tortillas

Optional: Avocado, Red Bell Pepper, Limes

INSTRUCTIONS

1. Preheat oven to 400°

2. Prep all of your produce. Chop potatoes, squash, onions & garlic.

3. Get two roasting dishes ready. Potatoes in one with a splash of olive oil & all the spices.

4. Make sure to toss the spices & potatoes together with your hands it is all part of the sensory experience.

5. Squash, onions & garlic in the other with a splash of olive oil & a little bit of salt & pepper. Place in oven & let roast for about 25-30 minutes.

6. While the potatoes & veggies are roasting you can wash & chop your romaine, cilantro, chives, red bell peppers, avocados & limes.

7. I mix the chopped romaine, cilantro & chives together with a squeeze of lime juice.

8. When the roasting is nearing its end, you can heat the tortillas over gentle heat. Assemble however you like & devour!

CHILI CHEESE FRIES

Prep Time: 15 min | Total Time: 1 hr 30 min | Serves: 3-4 Hungry Bunnies

Confession, I never had chili cheese fries until I made this recipe however, I promise you that these are delicious, spicy, crispy, hearty & so fun to eat! I personally loved these with some homemade cashew nacho cheese but you are welcome to use whatever you'd like. This would be a great finger food for if you are having a movie night, entertaining guests or just want a fun change of pace for dinner. So forget the beef chili, canned cheese & oily fries get ready for a dish that is so good you'll forget it's healthy!

INGREDIENTS

2 Tbs Olive Oil

6 Cloves of Garlic

1 White Onion

1 28oz Can of Diced Tomatoes + Water

1 C Carrots diced

2 Celery Stalks diced

3 Bell Peppers chopped

1 Tbs Cumin

1 ½ Tbs Chili Powder

½ Red Onion diced

1 Bay Leaf

1 Can of Kidney Beans

1 Can of Black Beans

4 Tbs Chipotle Adobo Sauce + 2 Chipotle Peppers

1 Lime Juiced

Nacho Cheese or Cheese of choice

Baked Potato Wedges

INSTRUCTIONS

1. Add 2 Tbs of olive oil to a large pot & let it heat up. Add in your sliced garlic & diced onion & sauté till fragrant.

2. Add in your carrots, celery, bell pepper, red onion, cumin, chili powder, salt & pepper & adobo sauce to taste.

3. Once everything has cooked down & become softer add your can of diced tomatoes, if you want this to be smoother then used crushed. Refill the 28 oz can with water or veggie stock & add it to the pot.

4. Bring everything to a boil & then toss in a bay leaf, 2 chipotle peppers, lime juice, & your beans.

5. Reduce the heat to a simmer & allow the chili to cook with the lid slightly covering for an hour. You can eat this sooner but I like to let all the flavors marry & allow the chili to thicken.

6. Grab your potato wedges or french fries & smother on some chili. Top with nacho cheese, or cheese of choice, guacamole, & whatever else you'd like.

GARLIC & CARAMELIZED ONION PIZZA

Prep Time: 15-20 min | Total Time: 30-45 min | Serves: 4-6 Hungry Bunnies

Mushrooms, caramelized onions, fresh herbs & cashew cheese is a match made in heaven. One of my favorite types of pizzas used to be a white ricotta pie with spinach & mushrooms, so when I decided to experiment with a white pie I thought I would add some new touches.

The balsamic with the onions makes the pie sweet but the cashew cheese makes it savory & creamy. I personally love to grill my pizzas, especially during the summer months, & this pie tastes great with a nice char to it.

INGREDIENTS

Fresh Pizza Dough (from the local pizzeria)

1 C Cashews

1 Tbs Nutritional Yeast

Juice of 1 Lemon

Salt & Pepper to taste

Fresh Dill

Fresh Oregano

8 oz of Baby Bella Mushrooms

1 Red Onion

1-2 Tos Balsamic Vinegar

2 Tbs Olive Oil (sub Truffle Oil)

Radish Sprouts

INSTRUCTIONS

1. Heat up your grill, and spread out your pizza dough on an oiled cookie sheet.

2. Once the grill is hot add your pizza & allow it to fluff up, but make sure that the crust just gets very lightly browned.

3. When the dough is fluffy & lightly browned remove it from the grill & set aside.

4. Make your cashew ricotta cheese by adding your cashews, nutritional yeast, lemon juice, dill, oregano & salt & pepper to a blender. Blend until desired consistency is reached & set aside.

5. Heat up 1 Tbs of oil in a cast iron skillet. Add in your onions & allow them to soften & become fragrant, about 3-5 minutes.

6. Add your mushrooms & 1 Tbs of balsamic. Allow them to caramelize together in the pan.

7. Begin to top your pizza, spread on some of the cashew ricotta & mushrooms & onions, grill till the crust is brown then top with fresh dill, red onion & sprouts.

INDULGE

BAKING + DESSERT

There is something special about baking, almost magical. No matter what age you are there is instantly a reconnection with the little boy or girl inside of us. The best part is that no matter what your level of cooking is, baking does not require a whole lot of skill. The deliciousness sort of happers & it feels like magic every time.

Baking is an indulgence. We don't ever really need to do it, even though in that moment it may feel like a necessity, but that is what makes it special. The exceptional thing about it is the ability to share it with others, to indulge together & share the satisfaction.

My favorite thing about it is seeing the light in someone eyes, seeing them smile & laugh & feel the magic. The smells, the love, the memories, the gratification, that is what is so special about baking.

These recipes are meant to be shared, they are meant to spoil someone you love, & most importantly they are plant based, which means you can eat all of the batter you want.

LEMON POPPYSEED MUFFINS

Prep Time: 5 min | Total Time: 45 min - 1 hr | Serves: 3-6 Hungry Bunnies

I would imagine these muffins being shared at a tea party, a tea party filled with fairies & all of your favorite stuffed animals.

As a little girl I loved having muffins with a little pat of butter & some fresh preserves. These mini little cakes are filled with so many dreamy flavors. Lemon poppyseed muffins with blackberry cream frosting are a sweet & decadent way to indulge in something special.

INGREDIENTS

2 C GF Oats

¾ C Coconut Sugar

½ tsp Pink Himalayan Salt

Juice from 1 Lemon (you may add more to taste)

1 C Water

½ C Coconut Oil + 1 Tbs

1 tsp Almond Extract

3-4 Tbs Poppy Seeds

1 C Cashews

¼-½ C Blackberries

1 Tbs Maple Syrup (optional)

1 Tbs Lemon Juice

INSTRUCTIONS

1. Preheat your oven to 350° & lightly grease your cupcake tin with 1 Tbs coconut oil.

2. Start by adding your GF oats to your blender & pulsing it until a flour forms.

3. Add in your coconut sugar, pink Himalayan salt, lemon juice, water, coconut oil, almond extract & poppy seeds.

4. Blend until well incorporate & pour into your pan. Bake for 30-45 mins. In the meantime make your frosting.

5. Blend your cashews, blackberries, maple syrup & lemon juice until smooth.

6. Let the cupcakes completely cool & decorate with your icing.

RAW CACAO MATCHA DONUTS

Prep Time: 20 min | Total Time: 1 hr 30 min | Serves: 6 Hungry Bunnies

At my grandparents house there was always someone who showed up with a fresh box of donuts. They came in a box with other assortments of pastries & they were always a big hit.

I was never big on them, in fact they made me feel heavy & sluggish but these raw cacao matcha donuts will never let you down. These are rich, decadent & light all at the same time, a perfect dessert for when the family gets together.

INGREDIENTS

1 C GF Rolled Oats

1 C Medjool dates

¼ - ½ C Sunflower Seeds

2 Tbs Walnut Butter

¼ C Coconut Oil

3-4 Tbs Cacao Powder

¼ tsp Pink Himalayan Sea Salt

2-3 Tbs Maple Syrup

TOPPINGS

Coconut Butter

Matcha Green Tea

INSTRUCTIONS

1. Add oats, dates, sunflower seeds, walnut butter, & coconut oil to your food processor.

2. Pulse everything until crumbly

3. At this point add the cacao powder, pink Himalayan salt, & maple syrup to the other ingredients & blend until everything is incorporated.

4. Press the mixture into a donut tin

5. Refrigerate for 1 Hour, drizzle with melted coconut butter, matcha green tea & enjoy with someone special!

*Side Note: The dates will blend best if you soak them for 45 mins to an hour.

HAZELNUT CACAO BROWNIES

Prep Time: 15 min | Total Time: 1 hr 15 min | Serves: 1-2 Hungry Bunnies

Brownies are my ultimate weakness. Whether they are raw, cooked, gooey, chewy, chunky or smooth I will always love them. These raw chocolate hazelnut brownies are probably going to be a problem. I say that because you are going to make them & immediately want to eat all of them, its okay, I have done it.

I love making these for friends & surprising them with something healthy that is made with RAW & REAL foods. I hope you guys love these as much as I do!

INGREDIENTS

1 C Hazelnuts

1 1/2 C Dates

3 Tbs Cacao

1/8-1/4 tsp Salt

Almond Butter

Cacao Nibs

Buckwheat Groats (optional for crunch)

Dehydrated Blueberries (for topping)

INSTRUCTIONS

1. Add your dates to your food processor & begin blending. If you'd like you could soak the dates before h& to soften them up.

2. Add in the hazelnuts, cacao, salt, almond butter, & buckwheat groats & blend until the mixture is sticky.

3. Remove from the mixer & pour onto a piece of parchment paper. I personally shaped it into a square shape using my hands & then wrapped it in the parchment paper.

4. Place into the fridge & leave for 1 hour, then smother them with almond butter & enjoy!

*Side Note: Before you attempt this recipe I would like to say that I highly recommend using a high speed food processor. The reason I suggest this is to ensure that everything blends properly. If you do not use a strong quality food processor then there is a chance it will over heat & even possibly break.

PEPPERMINT SHAMROCK SHAKE

Prep Time: 5 min | Total Time: 5 min | Serves: 1-2 Hungry Bunnies

This is a dangerously addicting shake that is both rich & refreshing. Who needs unhealthy shakes from fast food restaurants when you can make yourself a delicious & refreshing shake that is incredibly good for you! The cashews in this shake make it incredibly thick & creamy & the frozen bananas make it creamy like a frosty without having to add any ice. You can also use fresh mint in this recipe to really make it pop, whether you replace the spearmint extract or add to it.

INGREDIENTS

1 C Soaked Cashews

¼ tsp Pink Himalayan Salt

1 Tbs Maple Syrup

1 C Kale

1 Tbs Cacao Powder

3-4 Frozen Bananas

Water for Blending

1 Tbs Spearmint Extract

INSTRUCTIONS

1. Add all of the ingredients to your Vitamix blender.

2. Blend until well incorporated

3. Pour into your favorite jar & enjoy!

*Side Note: If you are using a Vitamix then you do not need to soak your cashews.

HONEY & LIME CHEESECAKE

Prep Time: 10 min | Total Time: Overnight | Serves: 8-10

Cheesecake is a mouthwatering, delicate, creamy & rich dessert that usually leaves a heavy feeling n your stomach. However, this cheesecake is special. Not only is it light but it does not leave you feeling bloated.

That is one thing I love about vegan desserts, they are much more guilt free without sacrificing any flavor! This honey & lime cheesecake is tart & sweet & can actually be made with lemon or lime. I personally loved the lime because I thought it added a unique flavor but it is totally up to you!

INGREDIENTS

1-1 ½ C Soaked Cashews

1 Tbs Honey (or Maple Syrup)

2 tsp Vanilla

¼ tsp Pink Himalayan Salt

Water for blending

1 Wedge of Lime

CRUST

½ C Walnuts

½ C Mulberries or Medjool Dates

Side Note: This cake comes out best when it is made using a Vitamix blender. The reason for this is to ensure that the cashews blend super smooth resulting in a very creamy & smooth cheesecake!

INSTRUCTIONS

1. Add the dates or the mulberries to your food processor & begin to pulse. Add in the walnuts & blend until well incorporated.

2. Press into your small cheesecake tin & place in the freezer while you prepare the filling.

3. Strain the water from the cashews that were soaking overnight.

4. Add them to your Vitamix along with the honey, vanilla, salt, & lime juice.

5. Blend on high & begin to slowly add in the water. Be careful during this process to ensure you do not add too much. You may also use a nut milk of choice.

6. Pour into cheesecake tin & freeze overnight.

CHOCOLATE CHIP COOKIES

Prep Time: 5 min | Total Time: 30-40 min | Serves: 3-4 Hungry Bunnies

Who doesn't love chocolate chip cookies? They are one of the most loved, go to desserts for people of any age. I have always loved my cookies extra chunky & kind of soft, whereas my dad prefers when they are kind of crispy & crunchy.

The smell always fills the house with such comfort & my favorite thing about this particular recipe is that these are a much healthier option & you won't feel so guilty about indulging in them! The coconut flour is better then other flours & this also makes these much lighter cookie overall!

INGREDIENTS

¼ C Coconut Oil

¼ tsp Pink Himalayan Salt

1 C Almonds

1 C Sunflower Seeds

3 Tbs Maple Syrup

½-1 C Dark Chocolate Chunks

1 Tbs Coconut Flour

Almond Milk for blending

INSTRUCTIONS

1. Add all of the ingredients to your food processor

2. Blend until well incorporated

3. If your mixture is too dry & is not blending properly then you may add Almond Milk for easier blending.

4. Preheat your oven to 350°, add parchment paper to a cookie sheet & begin to spoon on the cookies.

5. Bake for 20 minutes, then turn off the oven & let them sit to harden for about another 10-20 minutes.

Side Note: To be honest I am never fully sure how many cookies this recipe makes because it usually depends on how hungry I am!

CACAO SHAKE

Prep Time: 5 min | Total Time: 5 min | Serves: 1-2 Hungry Bunnies

The perfect dessert or breakfast shake that has you feeling like you just had a huge bowl of chocolate ice cream.

Did you know that cacao contains the highest plant based source of iron? This superfood is also full of Magnesium, which is great for a healthy heart & brain, has more Calcium than cow's milk, & is actually a natural mood elevator & anti-depressant. More of a reason to eat more cacao & enjoy every guilt free second of it, who's with me?

INGREDIENTS

1-1 ½ C Soaked Cashews

¼ tsp Pink Himalayan Salt

3 Tbs Maple Syrup

1 Tbs Vanilla

2 Tbs Cacao Powder

½ - 1 C of Ice

Hazelnut Milk for blending

INSTRUCTIONS

1. Add all of the ingredients to your Vitamix blender.

2. Blend until well incorporated.

3. Pour into your favorite jar & top with cacao nibs, coconut or whatever else you would like.

FRENCH BAGUETTES

Prep Time: 15 min | Baking Time | Total Time: 25 min | Serves: 4-6 Hungry Bunnies

There is something therapeutic about making homemade bread. The way the flour flutters into the air & forms a cloud while you gently fold in the ingredients, the march of your knuckles as you knead the dough, such a simple moment.

INGREDIENTS

1½ C Warm Water

¼ oz of Yeast

1 Tbs Honey or agave

4-4½ Unbleached all purpose flour

Pinch of Sea Salt

INSTRUCTIONS

1. Mix water, honey & the yeast & let sit for 5 minutes until the yeast becomes foamy then add 4-4½ C unbleached all purpose flour add a pinch of sea salt.

2. Mix together; the consistency will be crumbly but simply pour the mixture onto a floured surface & begin kneading out the dough. You want to do this for 5-7 minutes to be sure to get out all the creases.

3. Place the ball of dough into a lightly oiled bowl (olive oil) place in a warm place & cover with plastic wrap & a towel to contain heat. Let the dough rise & double in size for 1-1½ hours.

4. On a floured surface begin to punch out the air & let the dough deflate. With a sharp knife, separate into two balls & begin to form the oblong shaped baguettes.

5. Place on a lightly oiled cookie sheet & dust the tops of the bread with a little more flour. Create 3-5 more slits & then place in a 400° degree oven for 30 minutes.

*Side Note: My grandmother used to tell us that opening the oven during the baking process was bad, she used to really stress that! But I am certain that it is only a myth.

MINT CHIP CHIA SEED BARS

Prep Time: 15 min | Total Time: 2 hr 15 min | Serves: 8-10 Hungry Bunnies

I may have become obsessed with mint.

I have been adding it to so many desserts & I am loving every single way it has been used! These chocolate chip mint chia seed bars are very satisfying & feeling with super-foods & chocolatey goodness. These bars are refreshing, crisp, crumbly, crunchy & chewy.

INGREDIENTS

1 C Raw Shredded Coconut

⅛ C Raw Buckwheat Groats

⅛ C Ground Chia Seeds

8 Soft Medjool Dates

1 tsp Vanilla

1 tsp Peppermint Extract

Small Palm full of Fresh Mint

⅛ tsp Salt

1 tsp Matcha

¼ C Almond Butter

¼ - ½ C Oats

½-1 Tbs Cacao Powder

CHOCOLATE ICING

½ C Raw Cacao

½ C Coconut Oil

¼ C Maple Syrup

⅛ tsp Salt

INSTRUCTIONS

1. In a high speed food processor add in your dates & pulse until they are broken down & softer.

2. Add in the buckwheat groats, oats, chia seeds, cacao powder & almond butter & begin blending.

3. While the mixture is blending begin adding vanilla, peppermint extract, mint, matcha, & cacao powder.

4. Once the mixture is well incorporated remove from the mixer & begin pressing into a small pan.

5. Set in the freezer & begin making the icing.

6. Add all of the ingredients to a bowl & whisk until creamy & smooth.

7. Remove pan from freezer & pour the chocolate on top, place back into freezer for 1-2 hours.

DONNA CAKES *Donna Sammak*

Prep Time: 15 min | Total Time: 50-55 min | Serves: 6-8 Hungry Bunnies

---

This recipe is dedicated to Donna Sammak, a beautiful soul that I wish I could have had the opportunity to meet. This was one of her own personal recipes, it was always a huge hit & I wanted to share it in her honor. She used to make these for soccer games, holidays & bake sales but most importantly she would make them for her family.

INGREDIENTS

2 16 oz Chocolate Chip Cookie dough

2 8 oz of Kite Hill Cream Cheese

2 Bananas

2/3 C Sugar

1½ tsp of Vanilla

INSTRUCTIONS

1. Begin by greasing a 13" x 9" pan & preheat oven at 375°.

2. Line the bottom of the pan with your cookie dough mixture.

3. Mix the cream cheese, sugar, & bananas & beat until smooth, spread over the first cookie layer.

4. Spread on the second layer of cookie dough to create the top layer.

5. Bake for 30-35 minutes or until the cookie is light & golden brown.

6. Allow to cool completely, if you'd like you could refrigerate it prior to cutting.

Side Note: you can use fresh cookie dough or store bought pre-made cookie dough, it works either way!

PISTACHIO & ROSEWATER CHEESECAKE

Prep Time: 10 min | Total Time: Overnight | Serves: 8 Hungry Bunny

I used to love pistachio pudding but the one that comes in a little jell-o box that isn't very good for you. I have been experimenting with cheesecakes & variations of ice cream cakes & the more types of nuts I soak the more creative I get with flavors. What really brings out the delicate & subtle rose accent is soaking the pistachios & cashews in rosewater over night. I love this recipe, its so beautiful & truly a special cake.

INGREDIENTS

1 C Soaked Cashews

1 C Soaked Pistachios

1-2 Tbs Maple Syrup

¼ tsp Pink Himalayan Salt

1/2 C Rose Water for blending

1 Wedge of Lemon

Rose Water for soaking

CRUST

½ C Almonds

½ C Medjool Dates

Side Note: This cake comes out best when it is made using a Vitamix blender. The reason for this is to ensure that the cashews blend super smooth resulting in a very creamy & smooth cheesecake!

INSTRUCTIONS

1. Add the dates your food processor & begin to pulse. Add in the almonds & blend until well incorporated.

2. Press into your small cheesecake tin & place in the freezer while you prepare the filling.

3. Strain the rosewater from the cashews & pistachios that were soaking overnight.

4. Add them to your Vitamix along with the maple syrup, salt, & lemon juice.

5. Blend on high & begin to slowly add in the rosewater. Be careful during this process to ensure you do not add too much.

6. Pour into cheesecake tin & freeze overnight.

CHOCOLATE FROSTY

Prep Time: 5 min | Total Time: 5 min | Serves: 1 Hungry Bunny

Childhood memories often consist of eating some sort of fast food, even if it was just fries & a shake. Why not find a way to recreate a plant based version of the beloved chocolate frosty?

This frosty may be decadent, sweet, icy, & delicious, but the best part is that this smoothie is much better for animals & your waistline. Pair this with a side of homemade fries & you'll instantly be transported!

INGREDIENTS

1 Tbs Cocoa Powder

Almond Milk

1 Frozen Banana

Cacao Nibs

INSTRUCTIONS

1. Add Almond Milk, Cocoa Powder, & the Frozen Banana to your blender.

2. Blend until smooth

3. Serve with Cacao Nibs.

DONUTS & COCONUT CREAM

Prep Time: 15 min | Total Time: 45 min | Serves: 8-10 Hungry Bunnies

Chocolate donuts with coconut whipped cream icing? These are dangerous, decadent, fluffy, rich, chocolaty, sweet, moist & piled high with sweet frosty goodness. You can eat these with friends & bring them to parties & everyone will be super excited!

INGREDIENTS

2 C Self rising flour + 1 C for adjustments

1/4 tsp Pink Himalayan salt

2 tsp Baking soda

1 tsp Baking powder

1 C Coconut sugar

1 C Unsweetened cacao powder

2 C hazelnut milk or nut milk or choice (you can also do 1 C nut milk 1 C water)

2 tsp Apple cider vinegar

1 C Olive oil

1 tsp Hazelnut extract

1/2-1 C of Chocolate chips (optional)

Marbled Coconut Whipped Cream

INSTRUCTIONS

1. Preheat the oven to 350 F & lightly spray olive oil into your cake pan. Add 2 C of the self rising flour, pink Himalayan salt, baking soda, baking powder, coconut sugar, unsweetened cacao powder to your food processor. Pulse until combined.

2. Begin to add the wet ingredients. Add in the apple cider vinegar, olive oil, & hazelnut extract. Pulse the mixture about 2 times, do not blend just pulse.

3. Now you can slowly add the nut milk. This is important, you may not need the 3rd & final cup of flour if the batter begins to form & be creamy & smooth. Generally I add & adjust both flour & nut milk at this point (in small portions) in order to make sure the batter is not too thin or not too thick & clumpy.

4. Taste the batter & adjust sweetness if needed, I personally do not like a very sweet cake so you may want to add more sugar to your liking. You may also add your chocolate chips if you are planning to add them.

5. Once the donuts have completely cooled begin spreading on the marbled coconut whipped cream icing. Top with Chia Seeds & Strawberries .

PEANUT BUTTER CHOCOLATE CHUNK BROWNIES

Prep Time: 5 min | Total Time: 30-45 min | Serves: 8 Hungry Bunnies

Brownies with peanut butter & chocolate chips? I think I may have gone to chocolate heaven. Peanut butter & chocolate are a match made in heaven & these brownies are smooth, creamy, rich but light, fudgey, low in fat & gluten free!

INGREDIENTS

8-10 Medjool Dates

¾ C Almond Milk or Water

½ C Cocoa Powder

½ C Gluten Free Oat Flour

¼ C Vegan Chocolate Chips

1 Baked & Mashed White Sweet Potato

⅓ C Peanuts

3-5 Tbs Chunky Peanut Butter

6 Tbs Maple Syrup

1/2 C Coconut Oil

1/3 C Cocoa Powder

1/4 C Almond Milk

1 tsp Vanilla

INSTRUCTIONS

1. Preheat oven to 350° & lightly spray coconut oil into your pan & dust with cocoa powder.

2. Add the dates to your food processor, pulse until broken up & combined. Start adding in the almond milk, peanut butter, cocoa powder, oat flour, & mashed sweet potatoes.

3. Pulse until blended & well incorporated & then transfer to a mixing bowl.

4. Stir in the peanuts & the chocolate chips.

5. At this point you may taste the mixture & see if it needs more sweetness, if you then you can go ahead & add in 2 Tbs of maple syrup.

6. Bake 30-40 minutes or you can insert a knife & see if it comes out clean. If you want these to be fudgey then bake them for a shorter amount of time.

7. Add 4 Tbs maple syrup, coconut oil, cocoa powder, almond milk & vanilla to a bowl, mix with an electric mixer & spread generously onto brownies. You may also use butter for this step.

CACAO TRUFFLES

Prep Time: 10 min | Total Time: 1 hr 30 min | Serves: 3-6 Hungry Bunnies

By now you guys can probably tell how much I love chocolate. This recipe is a great way to utilize the left over almond pulp from homemade almond milk! I love utilizing the leftovers for things like desserts or granola bars it really adds a nice flavor!

INGREDIENTS

1-2 C Almond Meal

2 Tbs Cacao Powder

2 Tbs Coconut Flour

¼ C Water

1 Tbs Maple Syrup

½ C Walnuts

¼ C Sunflower Seeds

1 tsp Cinnamon (optional)

¼ tsp Salt

INSTRUCTIONS

1. Add all of your ingredients to a high speed food processor.

2. Blend all of the ingredients until everything is well incorporated & forms a ball.

4. Grab a table spoon & begin scooping out the mixture.

5. Form each scoop into a ball & roll in between your hands.

6. If you'd like you can roll the balls into cinnamon, cacao or pumpkin spice.

NUTS | SEEDS

Almonds

Cashews

Chia Seeds

Flaxseed Meal

Hazelnuts

Hemp Seeds

Pumpkin Seeds

Sunflower Seeds

Walnuts

SWEETENERS

Coconut Sugar

Dates

Maple Syrup

Molasses

Raw Honey

Vegan Dark Chocolate

BAKING ESSENTIALS

Almond Extract

Cacao

Cacao Nibs

Cinnamon

Ground Flaxseed

Peppermint Extract

Pistachio Extract

Pumpkin Spice

Vanilla Bean

Vegan Dark Chocolate

FATS

Avocado

Coconut Butter

Coconut Oil

Olive Oil

Sesame Oil

Vegan Butter

DRY GOODS | PASTA

GF Rolled Oats

Nori

Pasta

Soba Noodles

White Rice

SPICES & HERBS

Basil

BBQ Seasoning

Black Pepper/White Pepper

Cajun Creole Seasoning

Cardamom

Cayenne Pepper

Coriander

Cumin

Cumin

Dill

Dried Basil

Dried Oregano

Garlic Powder

Ginger

Mint

Pink Himalayan Salt

Sage

Smoked Paprika

Turmeric

WET | CANNED

Almond Milk

Beyond Meat Burgers

Black Beans

Chao Cheese

Chickpeas

Chipotle in Adobo Sauce

Coconut Cream

Coconut Milk

Diced Tomatoes

Hazelnut Milk

Kidney Beans

Kite Hill Cream Cheese

Kite Hill Yogurt

Liquid Aminos/Coconut Aminos

Matt's Kimchi

Tomato Sauce/Paste

FLOUR | MEALS

All Purpose Flour

Almond Meal

Baking Powder

Baking Soda

Bob's Red Mill GF Flour

Cornstarch

Hazelnut Meal

Oat Flour

Semolina Flour

RECIPE INDEX

ACKNOWLEDGMENTS

My heart is filled with so much love & gratitude for the following people. Thank you for supporting my kickstarter & helping this book come to life.

Rhonda D Floyd, Cora Ciaramello, Robert Pignatello, Octavio Avila, Angelo Rocco Ciaramello, Cora & Artie Ciaramello & Alanoud Alsaud.

Thank you to my beautiful friend Michelle Gerrard-Marriott for her thoughtful heart filled messages & continuous encouragement. You went above & beyond in supporting my journey. Thank you to Derek Sammak for always being my special taste tester, fellow hungry bunny & unconditional supporter. Thank you for your patience throughout many long days of cooking (where you did all my dishes), helping with editing my photos & even photographing on my behalf while I held sandwiches up from falling over.

Most of all, Thank You Jonathan Fidler for putting up with my slow & dying computer while you helped format, design & edit this book. I have so much appreciation for your criticism, sass & suggestions.

Made in the USA
Lexington, KY
02 October 2017